PRAYING WITH THE POPES

"This book offers a great way not only to learn about Catholic social teaching but also to truly understand how integral it is to our faith and how consistently it has been taught for so long. I quite enjoyed learning new things about our popes at the same time as I was being challenged to put into practice the ideals they have invited us to live out."

Fr. Dave Dwyer, CSP
Executive director of Busted Halo

"This book is a practical spiritual guide at an urgent time. As Catholics, we cannot afford to be cynical about politics and culture but instead must use Catholic social teaching to promote the healthiest kinds of civic engagement. As not just informed but inspired citizens, we can be instruments leading the way to heaven, the campaign that matters for eternity. Catholic social teaching is not about political platforms, but rather it is a tremendous gift of the Church to the world. *Praying with the Popes* introduces us to this beautiful body of doctrine and the popes who have formulated it. It helps us pray with these popes and begin to make Catholic social teaching the air we breathe intellectually, practically, and spiritually."

Kathryn Jean Lopez
Senior fellow at the National Review Institute
and religion editor of *National Review*

"*Praying with the Popes* beautifully reflects the clear and consistent teaching of our Holy Fathers for more than a century. These inspirational vignettes of wisdom and spiritual insights, highlighting the virtues of justice and charity, bear witness to the constant presence of Christ's love for his people. This book shows how the principles of Catholic social thought are woven into the tapestry of abiding faith and lived experience, and demonstrates how the Church speaks with one voice on relevant issues that promote and encourage human flourishing."

Deacon Harold Burke-Sivers
Author of *Our Life of Service: The Handbook for Catholic Deacons*

"*Praying with the Popes* is a remarkable companion for everyone seeking to deepen their prayer lives and their understanding of Catholic social teaching. By weaving together the voices of twelve popes, it offers timeless wisdom and practical reflections that inspire hope, peace, and faithful action today."

Inés San Martín
Vice president of marketing and communications
for the Pontifical Mission Societies USA

"*Praying with the Popes* helps you listen to our Holy Fathers over the last century and a half and get to know them. From the wisdom of Leo XIII to that of Leo XIV, through reflection and prayer, you can make the Church's social teaching your own."

Cardinal Michael Czerny, SJ
Prefect of the Dicastery for Promoting
Integral Human Development

"I spend much of my time chasing news, so it was refreshing to pause and pray with the words of these popes. A resource that offers much fruit for spiritual reflection on the Church's last almost 150 years as we enter into a new papacy."

Colleen Dulle

Vatican correspondent at *America* magazine

"Reading this book is like walking through the Vatican Gardens arm in arm with the popes, learning something of each one's personal story and papal pronouncements as you go. It effortlessly leads you through the paths of history of the Catholic Church during the last almost 150 years. A book that manages to both strengthen the intellect and sweeten the soul!"

Delia Buckley Gallagher

Vatican correspondent

"*Praying with the Popes* is great! It will help you meet our most recent Holy Fathers, learn about their lives, and engage with their ideas about how to care for others and create a more just and peaceful world. This book will help you pray, reflect, and study. And you will love the Church all the more because of it."

Most Reverend Nelson J. Pérez

Archbishop of Philadelphia

PRAYING WITH THE POPES

WORDS OF HOPE AND PEACE FROM LEO XIII TO LEO XIV

Introduction by Katie Prejean McGrady

Compiled and Edited by
Shannon Wimp Schmidt and Eileen M. Ponder

Ave Maria Press AVE Notre Dame, Indiana

Nihil Obstat: Reverend Monsignor Michael Heintz, PhD
Censor Librorum
Imprimatur: Most Reverend Kevin C. Rhoades
Bishop of Fort Wayne–South Bend
Given at Fort Wayne, Indiana, on August 11, 2025

Founded in 1865, Ave Maria Press is a ministry of the United States Province of Holy Cross.

www.avemariapress.com

Paperback: ISBN-13 978-1-64680-445-0

E-book: ISBN-13 978-1-64680-446-7

Special Edition Product Number: 30020

Cover and interior images information and permissions found on page 175.

Cover and text design by Brianna Dombo Nicholson.

Printed and bound in the United States of America.

CONTENTS

INTRODUCTION

BY KATIE PREJEAN McGRADY

For most of May 8, 2025, I sat in a tiny studio at the CNN studios in Washington, DC, monitoring and commenting on the papal conclave then taking place in Rome following the death of Pope Francis. It was early afternoon in Washington—early evening in Rome—when white smoke rose from the Sistine Chapel, letting the world know that the cardinals from across the globe had chosen a new pope. We watched excitedly as cheers and applause erupted from the crowd gathered in St. Peter's Square.

After waiting for what seemed a long time, my colleagues and I fell silent as Cardinal Dominique Mamberti stepped out onto the central balcony of St. Peter's Basilica, and the crowd fell silent. I fiddled with my earpiece, afraid it might fall out.

The volume was a little too low, and an aide kindly turned it up for me just as Cardinal Mamberti said with a wide smile, "Leone Quartadecima!" And that is how I, and millions around the world, learned that our new Holy Father, Cardinal Robert Francis Prevost of Chicago and Chiclayo, Peru, had taken the name Leo XIV.

It has long been a tradition of newly elected popes to take the name of a papal predecessor whose doctrinal and pastoral priorities the new pope intends to emulate. So, when I heard that our new Holy Father had chosen the name Leo, I was elated. His predecessor Pope Leo XIII is my favorite pope of the past century and a half. His pontificate stretched from 1878 to 1903, and he wrote the foundational text of Catholic social teaching in the modern era—the encyclical *Rerum Novarum* (*Rights and Duties of Capital and Labor*)—in 1891 as a response to the social upheavals brought about by the Industrial Revolution.

In *Rerum Novarum*, Leo XIII critiqued both socialism and laissez-faire capitalism and addressed the inherent dignity of the worker and the ways in which the conditions of labor often failed to uphold this dignity. He advocated for more widespread property ownership and just wages and reminded the Church of its role as a moral authority needing to address the social issues of the day. *Rerum Novarum* was released 134 years before Pope Leo XIV waved from the loggia of St. Peter's Basilica, and yet the principals in that encyclical formed our new pope and guided the ten popes between these two Leos.

Two days after his election, Pope Leo XIV met with the college of cardinals, no longer sitting beside the men who had elected him but standing before them. Not far from the room where he was elected, Pope Leo XIV shared his reason for taking the name Leo: "In our own day, the Church offers to everyone the treasury of her social teaching in response to another industrial revolution and to developments in the field of artificial intelligence that pose new challenges for the defense of human dignity, justice, and labor."[1] The seminal document of Pope Leo XIII's pontificate, one that bridged the nineteenth century and the twentieth and continues to inform the doctrinal and pastoral life of the Church, was the guiding force behind Pope Leo XIV's choice of name.

Rerum Novarum led to the establishment of Catholic social teaching as a distinct body of doctrine and theological inquiry. In it we can detect seven key pillars with which each of us must be concerned in large and small ways, depending on our own particular circumstances at any particular time. These pillars are: respecting the inherent dignity of each human life, promoting the sanctity of the family, protecting property rights, working for the common good, observing the principles of subsidiarity, respecting work and the worker, and pursuing peace and care for the poor. The Church is not isolated from the world; in fact, the Church has something to say about—and a way to be within and guide—the social systems and structures of our world.

Praying with the Popes offers you an introduction to the twelve men who have served the Church as pope from Leo XIII through our own Leo XIV. It'd be quite valuable to study in depth the biographies of each of these popes and to learn something of their contributions to the ongoing development of Catholic social teaching. It is also a worthy pursuit to reflect and pray with a few words from each of them and to consider how you might integrate their meaning into your own life. If we simply study, we're merely learning. But if we pray, we may just end up more carefully attuned to the heart and mind of God and the mission of the universal Church. Consider this book a primer on Catholic social teaching and twelve brief encounters with the remarkable men who have helped to shape and reinforce the social doctrines of the Church over the past nearly one and a half centuries. Each of the twelve chapters provides a brief profile of one pope and six quotes from him for you to reflect on and pray with. We've included simple prompts to help you. We hope that you will find many doors of interest and inquiry opening for you and trust that you will enter through those doors as time allows and the Holy Spirit beckons. We've identified for you the sources of the quotes, and we urge you to learn more and to pray more for the well-being of the Church and the world.

When our newly elected pope stepped out onto the center balcony of at St. Peter's Basilica on May 8, 2025, he introduced himself to the world with this simple greeting: "Peace be with you all!" He reminded us that this peace of the risen Lord is "a peace that is unarmed and disarming, humble, and persevering. A peace that comes from God, the God who loves us all, unconditionally."[2] What joy filled my heart!

As you pray with our popes from Leo XIII to Leo XIV, may you discover anew the hope and peace of Christ, which compels us all to engage the social ills of our day and move forward in making the world a better place for all people now—and for generations to come.

1.
POPE LEO XIII

FEBRUARY 20, 1878 – JULY 20, 1903

✠ PAPAL MOTTO ✠

Lumen in coelo ~ Light in heaven

Anyone who lives close to a century has stories of the many changes that spanned their lifetime. For Pope Leo XIII, born Vincenzo Gioacchino Pecci on March 2, 1810, the ninety-three years of his life were marked by some of the most expansive changes in human history. The sixth child of an Italian family of minor nobility, Pecci had a childhood marked by a Europe still predominantly ruled by monarchs, nobles, and aristocrats while agrarian communities dominated the landscape. Travel was powered by horses on land and wind-filled sails on the sea. He was nineteen years old when the first commercially successful steam-powered train began operating in England. The first ship to cross the Atlantic fully powered by steam engine set sail in 1838, one year after Pecci was ordained to the priesthood. The adult life of the man who would become Pope Leo XIII was fully immersed in the rapid changes brought on by the Industrial Revolution. This change was something he pondered with intelligence and discernment throughout his life.

When newly ordained, Pecci was tapped for diplomatic service at the Vatican and quickly promoted due to his adaptability and energy. In 1843, only five years later, he was appointed a nuncio (the highest level of papal ambassador) to Brussels, as well as ordained an archbishop. In Brussels, he encountered a parliamentary government for the first time under King Leopold I. During this time, the Vatican was somewhat skeptical of constitutional governments because it could not see how one could align with the teachings of the Church. Pecci, however, was persuaded by his time in Belgium and believed that Catholics could flourish under a constitutional system with freedom of the press. Unfortunately, after only three years, King Leopold perceived Pecci's intervention in some delicate matters as interfering and had him removed from the nunciature.

In 1846, Pecci was named bishop of Perugia, a minor diocese in Italy, where he was relatively ignored for the next three decades. Even though he was made a cardinal in 1853, the Vatican saw his discernment in avoiding conflict with the Italian government during the Risorgimento, or the Italian unification, as opposition to papal interest.

Thankfully, Pecci did not become bitter from this suspicion, instead choosing to devote himself to his own spiritual and intellectual formation as well as that of his priests. He chose to focus on drawing closer to Jesus and caring for those Christ gave him to lead. This spiritual depth and dedication to his ministerial calling was eventually noticed through his writings and highly regarded status in his diocese. His disposition and strength of commitment certainly contributed to his eventual election as pope in 1878, following the death of Pope Pius IX in February of that year.

During his papacy, Leo XIII was known for grappling with the issues that modernity presented to the Church. He reinforced the more conservative view that governments should ultimately be subject to the papacy but was openly sympathetic to scientific advancements and argued for a framework in which the Church and the state had different roles and responsibilities in the modern world. He rekindled the study of St. Thomas Aquinas as an example of how to bring faith and reason together without falling into tempting ideologies like Marxism, rationalism, and liberalism, which attempt to create utopias without God. Leo drew from the more rural past of his youth to try to bring centuries of the Church's Tradition to bear on a modern era that dehumanized and overlooked many in spite of its technological and political progress.

Leo XIII wrote many encyclicals addressing these types of topics, but none was more important than *Rerum Novarum*, or *Rights and Duties of Capital and Labor*, published in

1891, where he examined the impact of the Industrial Revolution and the need for justice within the working classes. *Rerum Novarum*, translated into English as "of new things," was itself a new thing because Leo directly addressed social issues of the day in it, rather than limiting his teaching to doctrine alone or to moral issues pertaining to the actions or behaviors of the individual. *Rerum Novarum* is considered the first document in the now robust body of doctrine known as Catholic social teaching. Leo XIII himself is often called the father of Catholic social teaching.

Rerum Novarum, though groundbreaking, was not the end of Leo's engagement with social realities. He continued to write apostolic letters and encyclicals focused on important discussions of the day. Using his political training, he directed major diplomatic efforts with various nations and attempted dialogue with the Anglican and Orthodox Churches. He also worked to support Catholic laity in their own organization of and participation in the various governments of the places in which they lived. Leo was the first pope ever filmed and also one of the earliest-born people to appear in a motion picture.

By the time of his death on July 20, 1903, Leo XIII was an international figure of great acclaim. There were more nations in diplomatic relations with the Vatican than at any other time preceding. The foundation he set for compassionately attending to the needs of the world became the blueprint for Church leadership in the modern era. When we think of what the pope does today, we're seeing the fruition of what Leo XIII was trying to achieve by addressing the social and political challenges of his day along with the spiritual needs of the Church. While our world has seen as much change since his papacy as he did in his ninety-three years on this earth, we are indebted to Pope Leo XIII's legacy of profound faith in God along with his deep engagement with the world and the continual development of its peoples.

WORDS TO ENLIGHTEN AND GUIDE

Rerum Novarum ~ Rights and Duties of Capital and Labor, May 15, 1891

Rerum Novarum, 45

Near the end of the nineteenth century, growing urbanization and industrialization left droves of workers in extreme poverty. Many were forced to brave dangerous working conditions, long hours, and little to no time off—all for insufficient wages. Although *Rerum Novarum* addresses several economic and technological ideas, the common worker, made in the image of God and redeemed by Jesus, is at the encyclical's heart. In it, Leo XIII teaches that the needs of those directly and even indirectly impacted by change must always be the most important consideration when evaluating economic innovation.

> Wages ought not to be insufficient to support a frugal and well-behaved wage-earner. If through necessity or fear of a worse evil, the workman accepts harder conditions because an employer or contractor will afford him no better, he is made the victim of force and injustice.

Reflect and Pray

Take a moment to breathe and open your heart to God. Read the quote again. What does God want for workers? What does he want for you? Pause and ask the Lord to help you see his vision for each person.

Rerum Novarum, 22

Leo XIII staunchly rejected communism and liberalism. Communism (also called socialism, or Marxism) holds that economic freedom comes from collective ownership held by the state. In contrast, liberalism says that only an unrestricted free market can create ideal economic conditions. Pope Leo reminds us that both are incorrect. We need property to care for our own needs, but everyone has a share in the goods of the earth. Only God's plan, which requires balance between individual freedom, the common good, and solidarity between social classes, can bring about true freedom and flourishing.

> No one is commanded to distribute to others that which is required for his own needs and those of his household; nor even to give away what is reasonably required to keep up becomingly his condition in life. . . . But, when what necessity demands has been supplied, and one's standing fairly taken thought for, it becomes a duty to give to the indigent out of what remains over. . . . It is a duty, not of justice . . . but of Christian charity—a duty not enforced by human law.

Reflect and Pray

Jesus tells us to "give to everyone who begs from you, and do not refuse anyone who wants to borrow from you" (Mt 5:42). This, wrote Leo XIII, is a duty of Christian charity. Where is God calling you to go beyond justice and give to those in need out of Christian charity?

Rerum Novarum, 24

In discussing the needs of the poor, Pope Leo identifies a central theme of Catholic social teaching: Whenever the poor and marginalized experience suffering, God favors them. Leo says that this scriptural truth, often referred to as the "preferential option for the poor," demonstrates that what truly matters is not wealth or success but compassion, goodness, and holiness.

> God himself seems to incline rather to those who suffer misfortune; for Jesus Christ calls the poor "blessed"; he lovingly invites those in labor and grief to come to him for solace; and he displays the tenderest charity toward the lowly and the oppressed. These reflections cannot fail to keep down the pride of the well-to-do, and to give heart to the unfortunate; to move the former to be generous and the latter to be moderate in their desires. Thus, the separation which pride would set up tends to disappear, nor will it be difficult to make rich and poor join hands in friendly concord.

Reflect and Pray

Consider what it means in your life to "incline" or lean toward those who are poor or otherwise oppressed as Jesus did. Who in need will you likely encounter today, be that materially, physically, or otherwise? Who is wounded? Exhausted? Lonely? Sick? Who is the most vulnerable in conflict? How can you incline yourself, your words, or your actions toward them in charity?

Rerum Novarum, 49

Labor unions were a new development in the 1880s and were often associated with radical ideologies like anarchism or communism. While many Catholics participated in unions, many others denounced them as disruptive to the social order. In *Rerum Novarum*, Pope Leo affirms labor unions that are peaceful, saying they uphold human rights and promote human development. When respectful of God's Law, unions move us toward a more just world.

> The most important of all [mutual-aid organizations] are workingmen's unions, for these virtually include all the rest. History attests what excellent results were brought about by the artificers' guilds of olden times. They were the means of affording not only many advantages to the workmen, but in no small degree of promoting the advancement of art, as numerous monuments remain to bear witness. Such unions should be suited to the requirements of this our age—an age of wider education, of different habits, and of far more numerous requirements in daily life. It is gratifying to know that there are actually in existence not a few associations of this nature, consisting either of [workers] alone, or of [workers] and employers together, but it were greatly to be desired that they should become more numerous and more efficient.

Reflect and Pray

What mutual-aid organizations or communities have helped you throughout your life and in what specific ways? Have any of these groups been connected with your employment? Did this benefit you? If so, in what ways? If not, why not?

Graves de Communi Re ~ *On Christian Democracy,* January 18, 1901

Graves de Communi Re, 16

This encyclical was written in 1901, toward the end of Pope Leo's life. In it, he addresses Christian democracy, a growing political and social movement that sought to align democratic governments with the Church's teaching. Here, Pope Leo details important principles that Catholics can follow in the public sphere and outlines the importance of charity in building up society.

> Nor are we to eliminate from the list of good works the giving of money for charity. . . . Far from being dishonorable for man, it draws closer the bonds of human society. . . . No one is so rich that he does not need another's help; no one so poor as not to be useful in some way to his fellow man; and the disposition to ask assistance from others with confidence and to grant it with kindness is part of our very nature. Thus, justice and charity are so linked with each other, under the equable and sweet law of Christ.

Reflect and Pray

We all have moments in life when we need help or find ourselves in a position to help someone else. How can we give and receive in ways that draw us closer to one another? In the quiet of your heart, ask God to show you one way to give and one way to receive selflessly and graciously this week.

Graves de Communi Re, 19

In the following quote, Leo XIII discusses another important theme of Catholic social teaching: the *common good*. This term refers to all the conditions of human societies that, when collectively met, allow everyone to flourish. Leo reminds us here that although it is the role of states to ensure this common good, all of us are personally responsible for contributing to and safeguarding it.

> For, no one lives only for his personal advantage in a community; he lives for the common good as well, so that, when others cannot contribute their share for the general good, those who can do so are obliged to make up the deficiency. The very extent of the benefits they have received increases the burden of their responsibility, and a stricter account will have to be rendered to God who bestowed those blessings upon them.

Reflect and Pray

Take a few minutes to write down or sketch what the common good looks like where you live. Where do you see people working together for the good of all? Where is more still needed? Tell God what you've noticed and how you'd like to see God work there.

2.
POPE PIUS X

AUGUST 4, 1903 – AUGUST 20, 1914

✠ PAPAL MOTTO ✠

Instaurare omnia in Christo ~

Restore all things in Christ

"I was born poor, I lived poor, I will die poor."[1] These words, spoken by Pope Pius X during his papacy, are hallmarks of his simplicity and humility. Born Joseph Sarto on June 2, 1835, he was the second of ten children of poor Italian parents. He carried his humble origins with him throughout his life, often eschewing the pomp and circumstance of the clergy, especially as pope. It was this humility and his deep love for Jesus that would eventually lead to his canonization in 1954.

The future saint found his calling to the priesthood early in life and was ordained in 1858 at the age of twenty-three. Sarto spent the next twenty-five years in service to the People of God as a parish priest until, in 1884, Pope Leo XIII appointed him bishop of Mantua in the Italian region of Lombardy. Just ten years later, he was made a cardinal and, upon Pope Leo's death in 1903, Joseph Sarto was elected pope. Early in his papacy, Pius is said to have cried at the extravagance of the papal court, telling friends it was a penance to accept the ceremony of his role—further evidence of his humility and solidarity with the poor.

Though more concerned about doctrine than social reforms when compared to his predecessor, Pius was interested in politics and justice. He allowed Catholics in Italy to vote in elections and ended the practice of governments interfering in papal elections. When France pushed back by removing the right of the Church to own property, Pius stood firm, insisting that the Church must be a voice for the law of Christ independent of the state. Pius also saw the gathering storm of World War I and worked diligently to bring about peace in an effort to avoid it.

Pius X wrote many letters and encyclicals addressing harmful philosophies of the day. But his writings were not his only work for justice in the world. He also organized relief for earthquakes in Sicily, sheltered refugees in Italy at his own expense, and condemned the malicious treatment of Indigenous Peruvians laboring on plantations. And, most importantly for the development of Catholic social teaching, he consistently pointed to Leo XIII's *Rerum*

Novarum throughout his papacy, reaffirming time and again its place as a binding teaching of the Church.

More than anything, Pius X wanted the faithful to grow in love for Jesus and know the truth of the Gospel in a changing world. He lowered the age for First Communion to age seven and encouraged all Catholics to receive the Eucharist more frequently. He took up liturgical reforms such as the restoration of Gregorian chant and updated both the breviary (Liturgy of the Hours) and the Roman Missal, the book of instructions and prayer texts for celebrating Mass. Pius also systematized canon law and reorganized the curia at the Vatican, which helped make the Church more responsive and efficient in the twentieth century. All of these reforms were meant to remove barriers that kept the clergy, religious, and laity alike from drawing closer to Jesus and practicing their faith in the world.

Unfortunately for Pius X, his work to promote peace could not prevent the outbreak of World War I in 1914. While he had foreseen the conflict, his inability to prevent it greatly disheartened him. He is reported to have said about the war, "It is the last affliction the Lord will visit on me. I would gladly give my life to save my poor children from this ghastly scourge."[2] Just a few weeks after the start of World War I, on August 20, 1914, Pope Pius X passed away, going home to the Lord he loved so well.

WORDS TO ENLIGHTEN AND GUIDE

E Supremi ~ On the Restoration of All Things in Christ, October 4, 1903

E Supremi, 7

In his first encyclical, given only two months after his election as pope, Pius X explains how he views his calling as pope in the modern world and addresses a few important social issues of the day. Among these issues are marriage, education, and preserving order and justice among the social classes. *E Supremi* lays out what the Church must do to bring all things under the authority of Christ.

> The desire for peace is certainly harbored in every breast, and there is no one who does not ardently invoke it. But to want peace without God is an absurdity, seeing that where God is absent thence too justice flies, and when justice is taken away it is vain to cherish the hope of peace. "Peace is the work of justice" (Is 32:17).

Reflect and Pray

Only in God can justice be realized. Only in God can we find lasting peace. Where in your life do you see justice lacking? Where do you see an absence of peace and well-being? Choose one of these to focus on in prayer throughout this week.

E Supremi, 14

In his first encyclical, Pius addresses the bishops of the world in order to clarify the roles of the clergy, religious, and laity regarding works of charity and justice. He reaffirms the importance and goodness of workers' associations (i.e., labor unions) and Catholic participation in them. He asks the bishops to ensure that these associations are first and foremost focused on religious aims, reminding them that, while the faithful should be concerned about caring for the souls of others, the clergy must be similarly concerned about ensuring that the laity are well-formed in the faith.

> But We wish that all such associations aim first and chiefly at the constant maintenance of Christian life, among those who belong to them. For truly it is of little avail to discuss questions with nice subtlety, or to discourse eloquently of rights and duties, when all this is unconnected with practice. The times we live in demand action—but action which consists entirely in observing with fidelity and zeal the divine laws . . . in the frank and open profession of religion, in the exercise of every kind of charitable works, without regard to self-interest or worldly advantage.

Reflect and Pray

When we care deeply about justice, it's tempting to make it our only focus apart from the Gospel. In truth, it is Jesus who gives us the strength and vision to make justice a reality. What spiritual practice can you begin or deepen this week to grow closer to Christ?

Singulari Quadam ~ On Labor Organizations, September 24, 1912

Singulari Quadam, 3

This encyclical was written to the German bishops in 1912 in response to questions about Catholic participation in labor organizations. Though not the last of Pius's responses to these questions, it is his last encyclical and the one that deals most directly with social issues, giving us excellent insight into how Pius X wanted Christians to approach social change.

> No matter what the Christian does, even in the realm of temporal goods, he cannot ignore the supernatural good. Rather, according to the dictates of Christian philosophy, he must order all things to the ultimate end, namely, the Highest Good. . . . All who glory in the name of Christian, either individually or collectively, if they wish to remain true to their vocation, may not foster enmities and dissensions between the classes of civil society. On the contrary, they must promote mutual concord and charity.

Reflect and Pray

When you consider and engage in social issues in your neighborhood, city or state, or at a national level, do you work to stay focused on the highest good, which is found only in Christ Jesus? Is your engagement rooted in mutual love and respect? Ask the Holy Spirit to build peace and unity within your family, neighborhood and among all peoples.

Singulari Quadam, 5

The German bishops wanted to clarify how, if at all, Catholics should collaborate with workers of other religions. Though Pius X was generally protective of the Catholic faith in the face of contemporary ideologies and other religions, here he also acknowledges the importance of collaborating with and on behalf of the common good.

> We do not deny that Catholics, in their efforts to improve the workers' living conditions, more equitable distribution of wages, and other justified advantages, have a right, provided they exercise due caution, to collaborate with non-Catholics for the common good.

Reflect and Pray

The common good belongs to every human being, not any specific faith tradition. How can you work with people across religious, social, and political lines to promote the common good in your community? Bring your thoughts, concerns, and enthusiasm to God in prayer.

Il Fermo Proposito ~ On Catholic Action in Italy, June 11, 1905

Il Fermo Proposito, 5

This encyclical by Pope Pius X was given on Pentecost in 1905 to the Italian bishops regarding the social movement known as Catholic Action. A European lay movement that advocated for greater Catholic influence in society, Catholic Action was present and influential in both politics and social actions. In this encyclical, Pius X writes to affirm the work of Catholic Action while also providing instructions for how the bishops should guide its activities.

> We have no need to tell you, Venerable Brethren, what prosperity and well-being, what peace and harmony, what respectful subjection to authority and what excellent government would be obtained and maintained in the world if one could see in practice the perfect ideal of Christian civilization. Granting, however, the continual battle of the flesh against the spirit, darkness against light, Satan against God, such cannot be hoped for, at least in all its fullness.

Reflect and Pray

The kingdom of God is breaking out in this world. But it will only be fully realized when Christ comes again. Reflect on the tension of "here-and-not-yet," a reality we live as Christians, noting that tension is required for something new to come into being. Bring your thoughts to God in prayer and listen to the Spirit's response in your heart. What might you be nudged to do this day to serve the kingdom of God?

Il Fermo Proposito, 19

While the Catholic Action movement was not a political party, many of its members were involved in political life and sought office in democratic governments. While Leo XIII had forbidden Catholics in Italy from participating in government, Pius X removed this restriction. In *Il Fermo Proposito*, he sets out guidelines for Catholics in politics and encourages them to stay true to their faith in Jesus.

> [It is the duty of] all Catholics to prepare themselves prudently and seriously for political life in case they may be called to it. . . . Above all else [a politician] must remember to be and to act in every circumstance as a true Catholic, accepting and fulfilling public offices with the firm and constant resolution of promoting by every means the social and economic welfare of the country and particularly of the people, according to the maxims of a truly Christian civilization, and at the same time defending the supreme interests of the Church, which are those of religion and justice.

Reflect and Pray

Not all of us will lead, but we are all called to work for the common good—the sum of social conditions in a society needed for each person to flourish as God intended us to do. How can your faith help you positively impact others in your community by advocating for the common good?

What virtues can you cultivate—with God's help—to do so? Ask the Holy Spirit to guard and guide you in these efforts.

3.
POPE BENEDICT XV

SEPTEMBER 3, 1914 – JANUARY 22, 1922

✠ PAPAL MOTTO ✠

In Te, Domine, speravi;

non confundar in aeternum ~

In Thee, O Lord, have I trusted;

let me not be confounded for evermore

Calling Benedict XV the "Forgotten Pope" reveals both his character and his importance in the story of the Church. Elected in 1914 one month after World War I began, Benedict, born Giacomo della Chiesa on November 21, 1854, in Pegli, a suburb of Genoa, Italy, spent his papacy working for peace while political leaders ignored and belittled his contributions. In spite of it all, Benedict continued to advocate for an end to the war as well as just and compassionate peace in the years after its end. While world leaders would not acknowledge Benedict's influence, it can still be seen in his writings and his impact on the Church.

Benedict's persistence was apparent from his early life. Born into Italian nobility with both Pope Callixtus II and Pope Innocent II part of his family bloodlines, he was born prematurely, resulting in a limp. This caused the young della Chiesa to receive his early schooling at home. He excelled as a student, and though his father wished him to marry and work as a lawyer, della Chiesa ultimately left his practice of the law to follow his calling to the priesthood. He was ordained in 1878 and was chosen to become the secretary to Mariano Rampolla, the apostolic nuncio to Spain. When Rampolla became the secretary of state at the Vatican, della Chiesa went with him, eventually becoming an undersecretary until his ordination as archbishop of Bologna.

When Pope Pius X passed away just after the start of World War I, many cardinals felt della Chiesa's experience in diplomacy would be invaluable during the conflict. He was elected pope on September 3, 1914, and issued his first encyclical, *Ad Beatissimi Apostolorum* (*Appealing for Peace*), just two months later. While he maintained strict political neutrality on the part of the Vatican, Benedict directed the Holy See to assist the suffering by taking such actions as establishing a special office to track prisoners of war, arranging for the care of the wounded, and redirecting huge sums of papal funds to humanitarian relief efforts.

Pope Benedict also increased the work of diplomacy on the part of the Vatican, which had become virtually nonexistent under his predecessor. As part of this effort and to maintain neutrality, he issued the apostolic exhortation *Allorché Fummo Chiamati* (*To the Peoples Now at War and to their Rulers*), which is now called his peace note. The exhortation detailed a seven-point plan for peace that many world leaders rejected because of its call for openness to territorial changes. This rejection was ultimately realized in 1919 when they left Benedict out of peace negotiations, even though his seven points had significant influence on the Allied parties.

Unfortunately, the 1919 Treaty of Versailles was extremely punitive toward the losing countries. Benedict warned against this approach, arguing that it would not lead to a lasting peace. But he was once again ignored by world political leaders. He spent the rest of his papacy trying to advocate for those affected by the war but was only able affect the most change within the Vatican walls. He died from complications due to influenza on January 22, 1922, leaving behind a legacy that many have overlooked but was foundational to the Church's teaching and continuous efforts on behalf of building peace.

WORDS TO ENLIGHTEN AND GUIDE

Ad Beatissimi Apostolorum ~ *Appealing for Peace,* November 1, 1914

Ad Beatissimi Apostolorum, 4

Pope Benedict XV released this, his first encyclical, just a little more than three months after the start of World War I. Often referred to as "the war to end all wars," this global conflict involved more than thirty nations, the largest war in recorded history. Technological advancements in weaponry lead to massive casualties at a scale previously unseen. It was in the midst of this horrific fighting that Benedict called on world leaders for peace.

> We implore those in whose hands are placed the fortunes of nations to hearken to Our voice. Surely there are other ways and means whereby violated rights can be rectified. Let them be tried honestly and with good will, and let arms meanwhile be laid aside. It is impelled with love of them and of all mankind, without any personal interest whatever, that We utter these words.

Reflect and Pray

Pause to think about where armed conflicts between or within nations are occurring today. Is there some action you can take to assist those displaced by such violence? Are there actions on behalf of justice in which you might participate? How is God calling you to peace in your own spheres of influence? As you contemplate, breathe deeply, and repeatedly pray, "Lord, make me an instrument of your peace."

Ad Beatissimi Apostolorum, 10

In this encyclical, Benedict XV states that the rise of conflict across the world is a symptom of increasingly secular governments that are disrespectful of religious truths. He saw the social ills of the time as proof that many world leaders had abandoned religious truths and thus created an environment where nations too easily cast aside what they owed one another in keeping the common good. In *Ad Beatissimi Apostolorum*, Benedict urges leaders to remember God's sovereignty and their responsibility toward all humanity.

> We remind the peoples of the earth of that doctrine, which no human opinions can change: "There is no power but from God: and those that are, are ordained of God" (Rom 13: 1). . . . Whatever power then is exercised amongst men, . . . it has its origin from God.

Reflect and Pray

No authority or worldly power is greater than God. No person, policy, or organization should ever come before God in our lives. Take a few moments to examine your conscience and ask Jesus where he should be sovereign in your life but is not yet. Invite our Lord into that place.

Ad Beatissimi Apostolorum, 22

After addressing world leaders in *Ad Beatissimi Apostolorum*, Pope Benedict turns his gaze to the Church itself. In addition to speaking on matters of internal organization and doctrine, he lays out how clergy, laity, and religious should understand and address the evils of World War I and work to bring about peace. The Church cannot fall victim to internal division but must instead act as a witness of its Savior to the world.

> The success of every society of men, for whatever purpose it is formed, is bound up with the harmony of the members in the interests of the common cause. Hence, We must devote Our earnest endeavors to appease dissension and strife, of whatever character, amongst Catholics, and to prevent new dissensions arising, so that there may be unity of ideas and of action amongst all.

Reflect and Pray

Do you see disharmony or even contentious factions within your parish or diocese? What impact does this have on the Church's capacity to be an authentic witness to Christ and to our faith? Are there any postive outcomes of disagreement or disharmony that you have witnessed? What were they? How can you work with conflict to bring about a greater good rather than turn away from it? Give over to God your hesitations, fears, or other reluctances. Pray for courage and calm in the face of dissension or strife.

Pacem, Dei Munus Pulcherrimum ~ *On Peace and Christian Reconciliation,* May 23, 1920

Pacem, Dei Munus Pulcherrimum, 9

During the yearlong peace talks following World War I, Pope Benedict XV wrote this encyclical, *On Peace and Christian Reconciliation*. He had long tried to persuade world leaders to create a treaty that would allow for rebuilding peace, but he was generally ignored because of the deep desires of the Allied nations to gain territory and punish Germany and its allies. In another attempt to influence treaty discussions, Benedict wrote this encyclical to advocate for the compassionate treatment of the losing side.

> Christian charity ought not to be content with not hating our enemies and loving them as brothers; it also demands that we treat them with kindness, following the rule of the Divine Master Who "went about doing good and healing all who were oppressed by the devil" . . . and finished His mortal life, the course of which was marked by good deeds, by shedding His blood for them.

Reflect and Pray

What does it mean to move beyond "not hating" or the simple respect of others and instead to act purposefully for their betterment? How can you do this in your everyday life, right where you are? Ask God for the gift of grace to love others selflessly and to work on behalf of their well-being.

Pacem, Dei Munus Pulcherrimum, 13

In this encyclical, Pope Benedict asks his brother bishops to guide the faithful in their dioceses to work toward reconciliation and to provide for those most impacted by the war. He asks them to follow Jesus's example in healing the "wounds of society" (*Pacem*, 11). In such times, when people must forgive terrible acts, it is the work of the Church to lead that effort.

> Therefore, Venerable Brethren, We pray you and exhort you in the mercy and charity of Jesus Christ, strive with all zeal and diligence not only to urge the faithful entrusted to your care to abandon hatred and to pardon offences; but, and what is more immediately practical, to promote all those works of Christian benevolence which bring aid to the needy, comfort to the afflicted and protection to the weak, and to give opportune and appropriate assistance of every kind to all who have suffered from the war.

Reflect and Pray

The message here from Pope Benedict XV will perhaps be difficult for many today to accept as Christian teaching. It takes great compassion and courage to stand against a culture that often tells us that revenge, or at least evening the score, is appropriate. The Gospel, the Church, and Pope Benedict tell us differently. Examine your current relationships. Are there people whom you want to ask for forgiveness or to forgive? Pray that the Holy Spirit guide you to do just that.

Pacem, Dei Munus Pulcherrimum, 14

In much of his writings, Benedict XV reinforces that peace must be built through constant efforts to overcome distrust and to increase the connections between nations. Even when it is tempting to seek vengeance, nations must work together for the flourishing of all if they truly seek the common good.

> The Gospel has not one law of charity for individuals, and another for States and nations, which are indeed but collections of individuals. The war being now over, people seem called to a general reconciliation not only from motives of charity, but from necessity; the nations are naturally drawn together by the need they have of one another, and by the bond of mutual good will, bonds which are today strengthened by the development of civilization and the marvellous increase of communication.

Reflect and Pray

Today, more than ever, we know that the destiny of people in every nation is interconnected. We can see, in real time, how decisions on one side of the globe impact people on the other. Take time today to pray for those in another nation, particularly a place where conflict or other tragedies are causing great distress. Pray for the people's healing and safety as well as peaceful resolutions of conflict and flourishing of the common good.

4.
POPE PIUS XI

FEBRUARY 6, 1922 – FEBRUARY 10, 1939

✠ PAPAL MOTTO ✠

Pax Christi in Regno Christi ~
The Peace of Christ in the Kingdom of Christ

Ven. Pope Pius XI was known in his time as a decisive pope who staunchly asserted the power of the papacy. He was a man of seeming contradictions who dictated commands to his clergy while at the same time making widespread reforms and defining doctrinal contributions to the Church. He was a strong advocate of increasing lay people's involvement in the life of the Church, the understanding of Catholic social teaching, and engagement between the Church and political systems and action. Pius XI took firm stances and spoke publicly against both Hitler and Mussolini, defending the Church against fascism, making him one of the most influential popes of the twentieth century.

Pius was born Ambrogio Damiano Achille Ratti on May 31, 1857, in Desio, a city in the Lombardy region of Italy. He was the fourth child of six born to Francesco Antonio Ratti, owner of a silk factory, and his wife, Angela Teresa. Ambrogio Ratti was ordained to the priesthood at the age of twenty-two and worked as a Vatican librarian. He continued his academic studies by earning doctoral degrees in philosophy, canon law, and theology and taught at a seminary in Padua, Italy. In 1919, Ratti was made apostolic nuncio to Poland, and in 1921, he was ordained archbishop of Milan. After the death of Pope Benedict XV, Ambrogio Ratti was elected pope and took the name Pius XI. The man who had often been seen as a quiet librarian and scholar soon became a lion of a pope.

Not long after Pope Pius's election, Italy fell under the leadership of Benito Mussolini. Pius negotiated with the Italian prime minister to create the Lateran Treaty, which established the Vatican as a separate city-state from Italy. He made similar agreements with governments in Eastern Europe, Mexico, and Nazi Germany. In spite of this initial diplomacy, Pius quickly became appalled by the racism and ideologies promoted by fascists and openly opposed both Hitler and Mussolini from 1933 onward.

Pius's commitment to cultural diversity became a hallmark of his papacy. In addition to his staunch defense of the rights of all humans, he nearly doubled missionary activity around the world and insisted on installing Indigenous clergy as bishops whenever and wherever possible. He also was able to reunite the Syro-Malabar Rite of South India with Rome. Less than a year before his death, Pius commissioned a draft of an encyclical condemning racism and explicitly denouncing anti-Semitism. Sadly, this encyclical was not completed before he passed away and remains in draft form to this day.

In the realm of social concerns, Pius pushed the Church toward greater openness to contemporary scholarship, science, and modern political systems. He founded multiple research institutes, including the Pontifical Academy of Sciences, and promoted the formation of lay movements to engage in political activity and social work.

Pius XI was forceful in his papacy in the internal affairs of the Church, an approach some saw as necessary in safeguarding the mission of the Church in a world torn apart by war, fascism, the rise of Nazi Germany, and the persistence of racism and classism everywhere. Pius XI reigned during intensely difficult and tumultuous years with a decisiveness many saw as dictatorial and others as urgent necessity. We can see how effective many of his reforms were in the way the Church operates today and the enduring strength of his convictions about asserting the demands of justice in a world torn by the severe lack thereof.

WORDS TO ENLIGHTEN AND GUIDE

Ubi Arcano Dei Consilio ~ On the Peace of Christ in the Kingdom of Christ, December 23, 1922

Ubi Arcano Dei Consilio, 33

Pope Pius XI's first encyclical, *Ubi Arcano Dei Consilio*, continues Benedict XV's focus on peace during ongoing recovery efforts and fragile relations between nations in the aftermath of World War I. It also examines the rapid social changes taking place around the world. Like Benedict XV, Pius reminds us that peace must be built through openness to and engagement with one another.

> First, and most important of all for mankind, is the need of spiritual peace. We do not need a peace that will consist merely in acts of external or formal courtesy, but a peace which will penetrate the souls of men and which will unite, heal, and reopen their hearts to that mutual affection which is born of brotherly love. The peace of Christ is the only peace answering this description: "let the peace of Christ rejoice in your hearts."

Reflect and Pray

St. Paul tells us in Galatians 5:22 that peace is a fruit of the Holy Spirit. When we are close to the Spirit, the peace of

Christ dwells deeply within our hearts. In fact, peace rules our hearts, as we learn in Colossians 3:15. How often do you allow peace to rule your heart? What difference does this make in your everyday life? Breathing deeply, repeat this prayer: "Come, Holy Spirit, bring me your peace."

Quadragesimo Anno ~ On Reconstruction of the Social Order, May 15, 1931

Quadragesimo Anno, 46

Promulgated on the fortieth anniversary of Pope Leo XIII's *Rerum Novarum*, this encyclical revisits themes of the common good and dignity of the person, reviewing them in light of the Great Depression and the rise of both communism and fascism in Europe. In doing this, Pius XI established a papal tradition of honoring important social encyclicals from previous popes by writing one's own to both commemorate the earlier document and further the Church's magisterial teaching on the same themes and topics.

> Twin rocks of shipwreck must be carefully avoided. For, as one is wrecked upon, or comes close to, what is known as "individualism" by denying or minimizing the social and public character of the right of property, so by rejecting or minimizing the private and individual character of this same right, one inevitably runs into "collectivism" or at least closely approaches its tenets.

Reflect and Pray

Think about your life and how you live it within a broader community and social order. How does private property contribute to the common good? Do you see any ways in which the common good is harmed by the use of private property? How well do you think your neighborhood, town, city, or parish keeps balance between the needs of the individual and the common good? How can you better form your own conscience about these aspects of Catholic teaching? Keeping in mind the teachings of Popes Leo XIII and Pius XI, pray for guidance from the Holy Spirit.

Quadragesimo Anno, 58

In this encyclical, Pope Pius XI discusses the importance of both commutative justice and social justice. Commutative justice is respecting the rights of individuals, such as not stealing someone else's property. Social justice is cooperating with others to ensure society is ordered to the common good, for example, collaborating efforts to pass laws that ensure workplace safety. Writing in the midst of the Great Depression, Pius applies this distinction between commutative and social justice to ongoing economic disparities of the time.

> To each, therefore, must be given his own share of goods, and the distribution of created goods—which, as every discerning person knows, is laboring today under the gravest evils due to the huge disparity between the few exceedingly rich and the unnumbered propertyless—must be effectively called back to and brought into conformity with the norms of the common good, that is, social justice.

Reflect and Pray

In a journal or in prayer, reflect on Jesus's words to the rich young man: "If you wish to be perfect, go, sell your possessions, and give the money to the poor, and you will have treasure in heaven; then come, follow me" (Mt 19:21).

Quadragesimo Anno, 137

Both fascist and communist dictatorships used popular policies aimed at restoring justice to gain power after the Treaty of Versailles was signed in June of 1919. (The treaty ended the state of war between Germany and the Allied forces of Europe.) The rhetoric of these dictatorships criticized faith as outdated and oppressive to what they called *real justice*, saying that charity numbed people to injustice. Like his three predecessors, Pius XI responded by reiterating the importance of charity as complimentary to justice. Pius reminds us that humanity always has room for and requires selfless love.

> Admittedly, no vicarious charity can substitute for justice which is due as an obligation and is wrongfully denied. Yet even supposing that everyone should finally receive all that is due him, the widest field for charity will always remain open. For justice alone can, if faithfully observed, remove the causes of social conflict but can never bring about union of minds and hearts.

Reflect and Pray

Take a moment to ask God for the grace to love without counting the cost, to see beyond hurt and injustice. Be honest about your hesitations and your hopes. Hold nothing back from our loving Lord.

Divini Redemptoris ~ *On Atheistic Communism*, March 19, 1937

Divini Redemptoris, 29

For more than a year, the Spanish Civil War had been raging. The conflict pitted Republicans, who included socialists, separatists, anarchists, and communists, against Nationalists, who were an alliance of authoritarians, traditionalists, monarchists, and fascists backed by Nazi Germany and Fascist Italy. During the conflict, the Republicans began directly attacking the Catholic Church. Pius, who was staunchly anti-communist (as well as anti-fascist), wrote *Divini Redemptoris* to refute communist ideology that removed God from human life.

> In the plan of the Creator, society is a natural means which man can and must use to reach his destined end. Society is for man and not vice versa. This must not be understood in the sense of liberalistic individualism, which subordinates society to the selfish use of the individual; but only in the sense that by means of an organic union with society and by mutual collaboration the attainment of earthly happiness is placed within the reach of all.

Reflect and Pray

None of us are cogs in a machine, although at one time or another, we have all likely felt as though we are. God loves us personally and has a unique destiny for each of us. Rest for a few moments, basking in that truth. Extend your reflection to those in your life who may struggle to see this truth. We are all intimately loved by Christ, the Father's gift to the world for the building up of his kingdom.

Divini Redemptoris, 27

Pope Pius XI takes up a key theme of Catholic social teaching in this encyclical when discussing human rights. Made in God's image, a human being is not simply a creature of the earth but also a spiritual being with free will and an eternal soul. As sharers in God's own life, all humans have inalienable rights that must be respected.

> Man has a spiritual and immortal soul. He is a person, marvelously endowed by his Creator with gifts of body and mind. . . . He has been endowed by God with many and varied prerogatives: the right to life, to bodily integrity, to the necessary means of existence; the right to tend toward his ultimate goal in the path marked out for him by God; the right of association and the right to possess and use property.

Reflect and Pray

In each person we encounter we ought to see a reflection of God. This is not to deny that people can become habituated to evil through their choices. Yet even then, the *imago Dei* (image of God) is present. When we truly see others, we see Christ. Pray with Jesus's words from the Gospel of Matthew: "Truly I tell you, just as you did it to one of the least of these who are members of my family, you did it to me" (Mt 25:40).

5.
POPE PIUS XII

MARCH 2, 1939 – OCTOBER 9, 1958

✠ PAPAL MOTTO ✠

Opus justitiae pax ~ The work of justice is peace

Ven. Pius XII was born Eugenio Maria Giuseppe Giovanni Pacelli in Rome, Italy, where he lived nearly all his life. His long reign of nearly twenty years spanned an extremely important and complex two decades of the twentieth century. Pius served as pope during the horrific destruction of World War II and global efforts to recover from this bloody catastrophe. His papacy came to a close at the beginning of the Cold War. He was witness to, and an active diplomatic player in, the earliest years of a new world order. He consistently advocated for fundamental human rights for all persons and the establishment of both international law and diplomatic institutions such as the United Nations.

One of four children, the man born Eugenio Pacelli on March 2, 1876, in Rome was familiar with the inner workings of the Vatican from an early age. His father, grandfather, and great-grandfather were all officials within the Holy See. It was no surprise that only two years after Pacelli was ordained in 1899 he was appointed papal secretariat of state, eventually teaching international law and diplomacy at its diplomatic school. He also served as apostolic nuncio to Germany from 1917 to 1924, first during Benedict XV's attempts to end World War I and later under the Weimar Republic. His time in Germany gave him a lifelong love for the German people, which many criticized when the Nazis came to power.

In 1930, then-Cardinal Pacelli became the Vatican secretary of state under Pius XI. While very different men—one cautious and one bullish—they complemented each other and achieved great diplomatic success. However, where Pius XI wanted to boldly condemn Nazism, Pacelli urged caution. That caution later led Pacelli, as Pius XII, to move away from Pius XI's resolute action on social and political matters.

Upon his election as pope during World War II, Pius XII adopted Benedict XV's World War I policy of official Vatican neutrality. But behind the scenes, he attempted to broker peace between nations and opposed the actions of both Mussolini and Hitler. Some found his public response to be so neutral that many, including his own cardinals and bishops, urged him to forcefully condemn Mussolini and Hitler's treatment of the Jews and other marginalized groups. Pius seems to have been concerned that public condemnation of Hitler would lead to more bloodshed in occupied territories such as Poland and France. Pius used his diplomatic influence and papal authority to protect Jewish people, provide direct assistance to refugees displaced by the war, and become an active, if not publicly vocal, supporter of the Allied resistance. Some today continue to criticize Pius XII for not using his position more overtly, especially once the Vatican was made aware of the horrors of the concentration camps. His legacy during World War II remains complicated. Allied powers were frustrated by what they saw as a public response too soft on Nazi perpetrated genocide, while the Nazis thought Pius an enemy and Allies sympathizer.

After the war, Pius worked diligently against communism, openly condemning the Cold War arms race and calling for an end to all nuclear weapons. He also encouraged Italian Catholics to participate in government to ensure democracy remained intact in their country. He published many letters and encyclicals encouraging peace and asking the bishops to work diligently against political and social injustice around the world.

Even as Pius encouraged greater engagement with the modern world, his health began to fail as the 1950s wore on. He became somewhat of a hermit, but at the same time brought about extremely important reforms and doctrinal pronouncements. In 1950, he declared Mary's bodily assumption into heaven as infallible dogma. Thanks to his encyclical *Divino Afflante Spiritu* in 1943, new Catholic biblical scholarship began to emerge using modern methods of historical and critical analysis. Pius also encouraged greater interreligious dialogue and instituted significant liturgical reforms, such as restoring the evening Sunday vigil Mass and reducing the fasting period before Communion. He even considered calling an ecumenical council to address the modern world, something that would be realized by his successor John XXIII.

Pope Pius XII passed away on October 9, 1958. His death marked a transition to a new era in the Church's approach to the modern world, much of which he had set into motion. He was declared venerable by Pope Benedict XVI in 2009, but his cause for canonization was put on hold by Pope Francis in 2014 due primarily to the lack of evidence of miracles. He remains a controversial figure in world history but also made important contributions to the Church and her social teaching.

WORDS TO ENLIGHTEN AND GUIDE

Summi Pontificatus ~ On the Unity of Human Society, October 20, 1939

Summi Pontificatus, 43

Pope Pius XII's first encyclical, *Summi Pontificatus*, was promulgated less than two months after Germany invaded Poland on September 1, 1939, marking the beginning of World War II. Since Pius XII maintained strict political impartiality about the war, as Pope Pius X had done during World War I, he did not speak directly against Nazism but rather made reference to its policies in more general statements like this one.

> And the nations, despite a difference of development due to diverse conditions of life and of culture, are not destined to break the unity of the human race, but rather to enrich and embellish it by the sharing of their own peculiar gifts and by that reciprocal interchange of goods which can be possible and efficacious only when a mutual love and a lively sense of charity unite all the sons of the same Father and all those redeemed by the same Divine Blood.

Reflect and Pray

Diversity is one of God's gifts to the world. Thank God for the gifts of your own culture as well as what you have learned from other cultures. Through the intercession of

Ven. Pius XII, ask the Lord for an end to division and hatred and exclusion and persecutions among nations. Ask for increased unity in pursuit of the common good. Ask for courage to do the work of justice that brings about peace.

Summi Pontificatus, 81

As did his two immediate predecessors, Pius XII wanted to see lasting peace in which all people could flourish. In *Summi Pontificatus*, he combats the propaganda being spread by atheist and dictatorial regimes. In addition to exposing the lie that the state is the supreme authority and end of human existence, he disputes the claim that peace can only come through the use of force.

> No, Venerable Brethren, safety does not come to peoples from external means, from the sword which can impose conditions of peace but does not create peace. Forces that are to renew the face of the earth should proceed from within, from the spirit.

Reflect and Pray

Peace proceeds from within. Peace proceeds from the Spirit. God's peace can inhabit your heart, a necessity for human flourishing and for the work of sharing the Gospel. Breathe in the Spirit's presence and open yourself to God's peace.

Summi Pontificatus, 109

Before closing *Summi Pontificatus*, Pius XII encourages the Church to hold fast to Christ as war spreads throughout the world. He urges Christians to persevere in kindness, charity, and steadfast witness to the good news of Jesus, much needed in times of strife. Above all, he reminds the Church that God is still working in the world, even when all seems dark.

> The world and all those who are stricken by the calamity of the war must know that the obligation of Christian love, the very foundation of the Kingdom of Christ, is not an empty word, but a living reality.

Reflect and Pray

Our lives should demonstrate to everyone around us that Christian love is not an empty word but a living reality that requires tending. Thank God for those who have been the living embodiment of Jesus in your life. Ask God how you can be the living reality of Christian love for those around you.

Summi Maeroris ~ *On Public Prayers for Peace*, July 19, 1950

Summi Maeroris, 12

Pius XII gave this encyclical five years after the end of World War II. Promulgated in 1950, the document speaks to a world forever changed by nuclear power and immersed in the beginnings of the Cold War. As during World War II, Pius confronts the claims that peace can only be ensured through an arms race.

> There have never been lacking, either in ancient or in more recent times, those who tried to subjugate the peoples by the use of arms; on the other hand, We have never ceased to promote a true peace. The Church desires to win over peoples and to educate them to virtue and right social living, not by means of arms but with the truth.

Reflect and Pray

God invites us to work with others through peace and persuasion to build a better world. Think about your immediate neighborhood and consider what needs are not being met within your community. What gifts do you have that might help? What graces do you need from the Lord to be a peacemaker in your community? Ask the Holy Spirit to bring them.

Sertum Laetitiae ~ *On the 150th Anniversary of the Establishment of the Hierarchy in the United States,* November 1, 1939

Sertum Laetitiae, 23–24

Celebrating the 150th anniversary of the first diocese in the United States, this encyclical was written just weeks after *Summi Pontificatus* in 1939. Addressing several issues specific to the United States, Pius XII spends time discussing an essential theme of Catholic social teaching: the importance of the family in society.

> It is also supremely necessary to see to it that the dogma of the unity and indissolubility of matrimony is known in all its religious importance and sacredly respected by those who are to marry. . . . This capital point of Catholic doctrine is of great value for the solidity of the family structure, for the progress and prosperity of civil society, for the healthy life of the people, and for civilization.

Reflect and Pray

Every family is different and no family is perfect. However, our communities are strongest when families strive for healthiness, happiness, and holiness. And families thrive when they have supportive communities around them. Ask Jesus to show you his vision of a community where families—and all people—thrive together. What does that look like? Strive to live into this vision each day.

Sertum Laetitiae, 40

In addition to pressing social issues, Pius takes up the topic of labor in the context of the Great Depression and its effects on the United States. He encourages the bishops to promote fair dealings by employers and bolster those looking for work. Finally, he turns to the topic of unions and their organization.

> But let the unions in question draw their vital force from principles of wholesome liberty; let them take their form from them, take their form from the lofty rules of justice and of honesty and, conforming themselves to those norms, let them act in such a manner that in their care for the interests of their class they violate no one's rights; let them continue to strive for harmony and respect the common weal of civil society.

Reflect and Pray

Reflect on the various organizations and communities in which you participate. Which ones help you grow in justice, honesty, and harmony? How do you see God working there? Do any organizations you belong to work against justice, honesty, and harmony? If so, are there actions you can take to help remedy this? Take your concerns and needs to the Lord. Ask for wisdom, courage, hope, and charity.

6.
POPE JOHN XXIII

OCTOBER 28, 1958 – JUNE 3, 1963

✠ PAPAL MOTTO ✠

Obedientia et pax ~ Obedience and peace

St. John XXIII, born Angelo Giuseppe Roncalli, is one of the most beloved popes of the modern era despite his brief reign of little more than four and a half years. John XIII is held in high esteem because of his jovial personality, kindly spirit, and love of the poor, but his desire to open the Church to the modern world is the distinctive reason so many Catholics consider him a great saint of our time.

Roncalli was born on November 25, 1881, one of thirteen children of a tenant farmer in the Lombardy region of Italy. Though he went to the seminary at the young age of eleven, Roncalli remained close to his family throughout his life, committed to maintaining the simple lifestyle they shared, even when he became pope. Though not a high-achieving student, he took to the life of order and prayer in seminary, eventually going to Rome for theological studies in 1900. One year later, his studies were interrupted when he was drafted into the Italian military, where he briefly served in the infantry. After ordination in 1904, Roncalli continued his studies and became a canon lawyer. He was made secretary of the new archbishop of Bergamo, Roncalli's home diocese, and, in addition to serving as the right-hand man of the archbishop, he spent nine years as a professor of theology and spiritual director at the local seminary.

When Italy entered World War I, Roncalli was recalled to military service, this time as a chaplain. He served as a stretcher-bearer, seeing firsthand the effects of mechanized war and decisions made by bureaucrats far from the frontlines. This greatly influenced his views on war, peace, and spiritual care for the individual. In 1918, he returned to teaching at the seminary, where he initiated new ministries and scholarly works. This brought him to the attention of the future Pope Pius XI, then the Vatican librarian.

As pope, Pius XI invited Roncalli to join the Vatican Diplomatic Service, making him a titular archbishop and assigning him as apostolic visitor to Bulgaria in 1925 which, though a minor role, required delicacy to protect the religious freedoms of the small minority of Catholics living in a predominantly Orthodox country. His skill in that position led to his assignment as apostolic delegate to Greece—also majority Orthodox—ten years later, combined with heading the papal diplomatic mission to Turkey, a Muslim nation. It was in Turkey where he would stay through the majority of World War II.

As World War II raged and the Nazis' anti-Semitic policies spread with each of their conquests, Roncalli saw the danger to the Jewish people and other minorities in Greece and Turkey. Using his diplomatic position, he arranged for thousands of transit visas to allow Jews safe passage out of Europe. It is estimated his intervention saved approximately twenty-four thousand Jews from the Nazi regime.

As the war in Europe drew to a close in 1944, Roncalli assumed that his role in diplomatic service was coming to an end. Instead, he was named the apostolic nuncio to the newly liberated France under President Charles de Gaulle, a particularly delicate post after Nazi occupation. Sentiment was high for retaliation against Nazi collaborators in France, including some bishops and priests. Roncalli also needed to address the many clergy who sided with de Gaulle and had become increasingly radical, as well as the many German seminarians being held as prisoners of war in need of release. Roncalli's interpersonal skills and calming presence were exactly suited to these needs in France, and he spent the next nine years working with the French government to rebuild. His success was so resounding that, in 1953, Pius XII named Roncalli a cardinal and appointed him patriarch of Venice.

Roncalli assumed that this was how he would spend the rest of his life in service to the People of God. He spent the next five years devoted to his diocese before leaving to participate in the papal conclave following Pius's death in 1958. Even Roncalli himself was surprised when, at seventy-one years old, he was elected pope.

Because of his age, most expected John XXIII to be a pope of transition, but the Holy Spirit led him to be bold in bringing the Church into a new era. Shortly after his accession to the Chair of Peter, he called for an ecumenical council, the first in nearly a century. He wished to see an *aggiornamento*, or updating, that would prepare the Church for the technological age. In 1962, he saw his vision realized when Vatican II began, televised for the world and showing a diverse representation of bishops from every continent. There is little need to describe here the impact of Vatican Council II on the Church.

John XXIII increased interreligious dialogue, opened channels of international diplomacy, spoke openly about political and social issues, and welcomed people of every stripe to the Vatican. His papal writings established important doctrine in Catholic social teaching and the pastoral understanding of the Church's mission. Yet, it was his holiness, kindness, and care for even the humblest of people that endeared him to the world, earning him the nickname "Good Pope John."

John XXIII did not live to see the temporal impact of his papacy nor the conclusion and fruits of Vatican Council II.

He died on June 3, 1963, to great lament across the world. He was beatified by Pope John Paul II during the Great Jubilee in 2000 and was canonized by Pope Francis in 2014.

WORDS TO ENLIGHTEN AND GUIDE

Ad Petri Cathedram ~ *On Truth, Unity, and Peace, in a Spirit of Charity*, June 29, 1959

Ad Petri Cathedram, 27–28

Written in the first year of his papacy, this encyclical outlines the vision that John XXIII had for his papacy and for the Church. It addresses both ecclesial and social issues and is particularly concerned with international cooperation and the tensions of the Cold War. Here, John XXIII appeals to our common humanity.

> We are called brothers. We actually are brothers. We share a common destiny in this life and the next. Why, then, do we act as though we are foes and enemies? Why do we envy one another? Why do we stir up hatred? Why do we ready lethal weapons for use against our brothers? There has already been enough warfare among men!

Reflect and Pray

In the spirit of Good Pope John, examine your day or your week in light of this quote. Ask yourself: *Have I treated those around me as beloved brothers and sisters? Or have I looked on them as roadblocks to what I want? Have I viewed them with envy or resentment and stirred up ill will between us? Have I participated in demeaning or hateful behavior, even if just following the crowd? Have I neglected my sisters and brothers who lack what they need to flourish?* Pray through the intercession of St. John XIII to receive the graces you need to love as Christ would have us love.

Mater et Magistra ~ On Christianity and Social Progress, May 14, 1961

Mater et Magistra, 83

Pope John XXII began this encyclical on social progress with these words: "Mother and Teacher [*Mater et Magistra*] of all nations—such is the Catholic Church in the mind of her Founder, Jesus Christ." He refers to Christianity as the "meeting-point of earth and heaven" and lays the foundation of our responsibilities toward care of body and soul of our fellow human beings.

> Consequently, if the whole structure and organization of an economic system is such as to compromise human dignity, to lessen a man's sense of responsibility or rob him of opportunity for exercising personal initiative, then such a system, We maintain, is altogether unjust—no matter how much wealth it produces, or how justly and equitably such wealth is distributed.

Reflect and Pray

John XXIII reminds us that there is more to life than relieving our material needs. We need space to create, dream, connect, and care for one another. How can you create and dream along with God this week? How can you join God in love and care of others?

Mater et Magistra, 236

One of the most important themes of *Mater et Magistra* is the principle of subsidiarity. This is the belief that power, goods, ownership, and decision-making should stay at the most individual or local level first and only be assumed by the state if necessary for the common good. To put this and other principles into practice, John XXIII describes a now-popular approach of discernment, commonly known as the "See-Judge-Act" method today.

> There are three stages which should normally be followed in the reduction of social principles into practice. First, one reviews the concrete situation; secondly, one forms a judgment on it in the light of these same principles; thirdly, one decides what in the circumstances can and should be done to implement these principles. These are the three stages that are usually expressed in the three terms: look, judge, act.

Reflect and Pray

Try the "See-Judge-Act" method in your own life. Identify a situation that needs discernment and action. Ask God to show you how the Gospel speaks to this matter and what possible responses (since solutions are not always immediately apparent) are nearest to the truth of the Gospel. Finally, listen to the Holy Spirit and decide what action you will take.

Pacem in Terris ~ On Establishing Universal Peace in Truth, Justice, Charity, and Liberty, April 11, 1963

Pacem in Terris, 28

This final encyclical of John XXII focused on peace-building and global solidarity. Throughout it, John expounds upon a major theme of Catholic social teaching: human rights and their corresponding responsibilities.

> The natural rights of which We have so far been speaking are inextricably bound up with as many duties, all applying to one and the same person. These rights and duties derive their origin, their sustenance, and their indestructibility from the natural law, which in conferring the one imposes the other.

Reflect and Pray

We often focus on individual rights and forget that those rights come with corresponding responsibilities, which Pope John tells us are inseparable from those rights. A good example of this is the right to food and the Christian responsibility to feed the hungry. Look at your own relationships, both personal and beyond, and ask God to show you where you have responsibilities to work for the good of others. Invite the Lord to show you specific people and situations where you can be the presence of Christ by exercising a right while assuming the responsibility that right brings.

Pacem in Terris, 131

John XXIII wrote *Pacem in Terris* just a few months after the Cuban Missile Crisis between Russia and the United States, when he was ailing and close to the end of his life. John boldly calls for nuclear disarmament and speaks of the importance of building peace through consistent collaboration and good faith. He calls not just leaders, but all people, to think globally when considering the common good.

> From this it is clear that no state can fittingly pursue its own interests in isolation from the rest, nor, under such circumstances, can it develop itself as it should. The prosperity and progress of any state is in part consequence, and in part cause, of the prosperity and progress of all other states.

Reflect and Pray

Most of us are not world leaders, but we can still think globally about our actions. In conversation with the Lord, reflect on your daily life and habits. How do they impact people in other parts of the world? In what ways have they been made possible by other nations and their people? In what ways do you contribute positively or negatively to the local, national, and global community?

Pacem in Terris, 165

A hallmark of John XXIII's life was his ability to build peace in all his encounters. Drawing from his own experiences—from growing up with twelve siblings in a small village in Lombardy to carrying the wounded off battlefields and rebuilding a devastated and divided France—he tells us how peace reigns on earth. Peace comes from a heart close to Christ, who himself is our peace (Eph 2:14).

> The world will never be the dwelling place of peace, till peace has found a home in the heart of each and every man, till every man preserves in himself the order ordained by God to be preserved.

Reflect and Pray

Take a few moments of silence to breathe deeply and invite the Holy Spirit into your heart. After a few breaths, repeat this prayer: "Jesus, Son of the Living God, be my peace."

7.
POPE PAUL VI

JUNE 21, 1963 – AUGUST 6, 1978

✻ PAPAL MOTTO ✻

Cum Ipso in monte ~
With Him on the mountain

It's no surprise that the pope who began making apostolic visits around the globe and was known as the "archbishop of the workers" was the son of a socially and politically active couple. St. Paul VI was born Giovanni Battista Montini in Italy on September 26, 1897, to Giorgio and Giuditta Alghisi. His father was a lawyer who eventually became a member of the Italian Parliament, and his mother was an active member of Catholic Action in Italy. The second of three sons, Montini followed his vocation to the priesthood, becoming ordained in 1920 and entering graduate studies that would eventually lead him to the Vatican's

Secretariat of State, where he worked from 1924 until his ordination as archbishop of Milan in 1954.

Montini brought the formation he received in seminary and the influence of his upbringing into all of his work. This became most apparent during his time leading the Archdiocese of Milan. In that episcopate, Montini began to employ new methods of evangelization, especially to reach workers disaffected with the Church and its response to the urgent and changing needs of the modern period. Montini would frequently visit factories in an effort to build relationships with workers and focused on issues that mattered to them. He addressed immigration and labor issues in particular, especially in trying to combat the growing materialism and communism that followed the devastation of World War II.

Though Montini refused an initial invitation to be appointed a cardinal in 1953, he was eventually elevated to the College of Cardinals by Pope John XXIII in 1958. He enthusiastically assisted Pope John in preparing for and participating in Vatican Council II. After John XXIII died in 1963, Montini was elected pope and became Paul VI. He immediately confirmed the decision to continue Vatican Council II, guiding the next three sessions with his pastoral and diplomatic experience and academic expertise to help the bishops bridge the Church's Tradition with its need to meet the missionary moment.

After the council, Paul VI found himself with the delicate task of navigating the global Church through the new reforms. He began this work the day that the council closed by announcing, in coordination with the ecumenical patriarch of Constantinople, Athenagoras, that the mutual excommunication imposed by the Catholic and Orthodox Churches during the Great Schism of 1054 was now lifted. He followed this action over the next decade by meeting with Athenagoras, other patriarchs, and Protestant Christian leaders to move toward healing the rifts among Christians around the world.

In addition, Paul VI began the modern tradition of globetrotting apostolic visits. He became the first pope to set foot on every continent, making journeys to North and South America, Africa, and Asia to encourage the Catholic communities in those regions, further interdenominational dialogue, and speak on issues of social justice, peace, international cooperation, and human rights. As part of this work, he established a permanent observer at the United Nations from the Vatican, affirming John XXIII's commitment to building lasting world peace. At the same time, he undertook reforms to canon law regarding marriage, the terms and roles of bishops and cardinals, and the liturgical and theological reforms instructed by Vatican Council II. Paul VI, often unfairly criticized for his cautious approach to decision-making, led the Church with forethought, discernment, and courage through its most momentous period of change since the Protestant Reformation.

We can see Paul VI's visionary understanding of the Church's mission more fully in his apostolic writings. Most address social problems in some way (including challenges to traditional Church teachings on such issues as marriage and priestly celibacy) and all shed light on a man who was deeply compassionate for the widespread flock under his care. In the twenty-first century, the apostolic exhortation *Evangelii Nuntiandi* and the encyclical *Populorum Progressio* are considered his two most influential works. *Evangelii Nuntiandi* (*On Evangelization in the Modern World*) is a broad look at effective preaching of the Gospel that speaks of the importance of relationship, cultural exchange, and social issues as part of evangelization. *Populorum Progressio* (*On the Development of Peoples*) discusses economic affairs, social justice, and global peace in light of *integral human development*—that is, development that considers the whole of human life and the good of the human person.

Paul VI died on August 6, 1978, leaving behind a Church engaged with the modern world, just as his predecessor John XXIII envisioned. In 2014, Paul VI was beatified by Pope Francis and then canonized four years later. This great saint exemplified what it means to be a disciple who works diligently to bring the Good News of Jesus Christ to a diverse and rapidly changing world. He is a shining example for those of us living in a similar world to have compassion and care for every human being, all of whom are loved beyond measure by God.

WORDS TO ENLIGHTEN AND GUIDE

Populorum Progressio ~ On the Development of Peoples, March 26, 1967

Populorum Progressio, 17

This encyclical was promulgated in 1967 amid a turbulent decade of rapid change. Paul VI introduces the idea of *integral human development*, which draws significantly from and expands on Pope Pius X's writings on solidarity. Paul calls the Church to think more globally about human rights and progress by bringing the light of the Gospel to new and challenging problems around the world.

> We are the heirs of earlier generations, and we reap benefits from the efforts of our contemporaries; we are under obligation to all [people]. Therefore we cannot disregard the welfare of those who will come after us to increase the human family. The reality of human solidarity brings us not only benefits but also obligations.

Reflect and Pray

Reflect on the benefits and values that have been passed on to you from previous generations. Consider which you would like to pass on to future generations. Bring your reflections to God in prayer.

Populorum Progressio, 35

After World War II, the technological and social progress of some nations far outstripped the majority—especially disadvantaging the global south. Paul VI, who had traveled much of the world during his apostolic visits, calls attention to this reality throughout *Populorum Progressio* and invites the Church to global action. He urges a holistic view of progress based in the kinship of all humanity.

> We can even say that economic growth is dependent on social progress, the goal to which it aspires; and that basic education is the first objective for any nation seeking to develop itself. Lack of education is as serious as lack of food; the illiterate is a starved spirit.

Reflect and Pray

Human life is not simply about meeting basic needs. We are made to create and to be in relationship with God and one another. What are your creative, relational, and spiritual needs? Your community's needs? What do you and those around you need to truly thrive?

Populorum Progressio, 47

Many consider *Populorum Progressio* to be Pope Paul VI's attempt to apply *Gaudium et Spes*, Vatican Council II's Pastoral Constitution, to the social realities he observed. In *Populorum Progressio*, Paul is "scrutinizing the signs of the times and of interpreting them in the light of the Gospel."[1] He paints a picture of a world transformed by Jesus Christ and challenges us to go beyond justice toward true human flourishing.

> It is not just a question of eliminating hunger and reducing poverty. It is not just a question of fighting wretched conditions, though this is an urgent and necessary task. It involves building a human community where [everyone] can live truly human lives, free from discrimination on account of race, religion or nationality, free from servitude to other[s] . . . or to natural forces which they cannot yet control satisfactorily. It involves building a human community where liberty is not an idle word, where the needy Lazarus can sit down with the rich man at the same banquet table.

Reflect and Pray

Picture your community sitting at a banquet table. Who is welcomed and celebrated? Who is excluded? Who chooses not to sit? Why? If Jesus were to come to the table, how would he react? Take some time to listen and respond to the Lord.

Populorum Progressio, 86

At the time it was promulgated, many traditionalists within the Church saw *Populorum Progressio* as radical and possibly even Marxist. Paul VI faced similar backlash from progressive Catholics over other encyclicals and exhortations of his. Instead of backing down in the face of criticism, he continued to ask the Church to love Christ, cultivate virtue, and love our neighbors as ourselves.

> Genuine progress does not consist in wealth sought for personal comfort or for its own sake; rather it consists in an economic order designed for the welfare of the human person, where the daily bread that each [person] receives reflects the glow of brotherly love and the helping hand of God.

Reflect and Pray

In a journal or conversation with God, reflect on what it means to pray the words "Give us this day our daily bread." What does it mean to trust God for your daily needs? How do you know when you have enough? What is Jesus saying to you personally?

Evangelii Nuntiandi ~ On Evangelization in the Modern World, December 8, 1975

Evangelii Nuntiandi, 29

As an apostolic exhortation, *Evangelii Nuntiandi* does not provide new doctrine on evangelization. It is, rather, Paul VI's encouragement to evangelize with new methods. Though not specifically addressing Catholic social teaching, Paul is concerned with several social issues because he recognizes that the Good News of Jesus is not only for one's spiritual life but for all aspects of life. And these are redeemed and renewed by the life, death, and resurrection of Christ.

> But evangelization would not be complete if it did not take account of the unceasing interplay of the Gospel and of [one's] concrete life, both personal and social. This is why evangelization involves an explicit message, adapted to the different situations constantly being realized, about the rights and duties of every human being, about family life without which personal growth and development is hardly possible, . . . about life in society, about international life, peace, justice and development—a message especially energetic today about liberation.

Reflect and Pray

Jesus cares about every facet of human life. There is no part of the world he does not want to redeem. He wants to bring healing to every person, every relationship, every community. Silently rest in the Lord's presence, inviting his liberating presence into your heart and our world.

Evangelii Nuntiandi, 36

Liberation theology was a new approach to theology in the 1960s that read the Gospel in light of the experiences of colonized populations. The liberation theology movement includes a wide spectrum of thinkers, some of whom equated the Kingdom of God with specific political and economic systems. In *Evangelii Nuntiandi*, Paul VI rejects this particular view while affirming other aspects of liberation theology that add to the Church's rich tradition of evangelization and social justice.

> The Church considers it to be undoubtedly important to build up structures which are more human, more just, more respectful of the rights of the person and less oppressive and less enslaving, but she is conscious that the best structures and the most idealized systems soon become inhuman if the inhuman inclinations of the human heart are not made wholesome, if those who live in these structures or who rule them do not undergo a conversion of heart and of outlook.

Reflect and Pray

Justice is an essential aspect of following Christ. But only our ongoing individual and communal commitment to conversion of heart can truly bring about God's Kingdom. Take a few moments of silence, then repeat the following prayer: "Create in me a clean heart, O God" (Ps 51:10).

8.
POPE JOHN PAUL I

AUGUST 26, 1978 – SEPTEMBER 28, 1978

✠ PAPAL MOTTO ✠

Humilitas ~ Humility

Well-known for having the shortest pontificate in modern history, Bl. John Paul I is remembered by those who knew him as a pastoral and happy man. Called "the Smiling Pope," John Paul drew in ordinary people with his warmth and ability to communicate the faith in an accessible way. He was extremely dedicated to workers, the poor, and the marginalized. Known for his kindness, he was also an extremely humble and approachable man who adopted one word—*Humilitas*—as his papal motto.

That kindness and humility was visible from an early age. Born Albino Luciani on October 17, 1912, he was extremely intelligent, eventually mastering six languages.

His mother, Bortola, a devout Catholic, encouraged him to read widely and taught him the faith with gentleness and simplicity. Luciani later credited much of his faith to his mother's influence and instruction. His father, Giovanni, on the other hand, was a bricklayer and socialist who was skeptical of the Church. Yet when Luciani chose to enter the seminary, his father reluctantly gave him permission. His father only asked that, as a priest, he take the part of the workers and the poor because "that is what Christ did."[1]

After his ordination at twenty-two years old, Luciani was briefly assigned as a curate before becoming a seminary professor. He taught seminary for decades until he was unexpectedly named bishop of Vittorio Veneto in 1958 by John XXIII, who knew Luciani from John's days as patriarch of Venice. Luciani spent the next decade trying to faithfully serve his flock, often interceding in labor disputes and working to reform the clergy within his diocese. During his time in Vittorio Veneto, Luciani participated in Vatican Council II and was deeply moved by the experience. He frequently defended the work of the council within his diocese and supported Pope Paul VI's efforts to interpret the council throughout Paul's papacy.

In 1969, Pope Paul VI assigned Luciani as patriarch of Venice and elevated him to the College of Cardinals. Luciani continued his dedication to the poor and to social issues, including establishing family counseling clinics to assist the poor in dealing with financial and marital challenges. During that time, he wrote a book of essays titled *Illustrissimi* (*The Illustrious Ones*), which is a series of imaginative letters to historical and fictional figures. Translated into multiple languages, *Illustrissimi*, along with his simple catechism called *Catechetica in Briciole* (*Catechism in Crumbs*), has been published many times over and read throughout the world. Both speak to Luciani's sense of humor, intelligence, and desire to share the love of Jesus in a way that all could understand.

When Paul VI passed away, Luciani came to the conclave expecting to vote and head back to Venice. But the cardinals seemingly wanted a simple, cheerful man like John XXXIII as their next pontiff. When Luciani was elected, he was reported to have been shocked. Yet, he simply smiled and said to his brother cardinals, "May God forgive you for what you have done."[2] Upon accepting the Chair of Peter, he chose the name John Paul, the first double name in papal history, to honor both John XXIII and Paul VI. In his Angelus address the following day, he stated, "I have neither the 'wisdom of the heart' of Pope John, nor the preparation and culture of Pope Paul, but I am in their place. I must seek to serve the Church. I hope that you will help me with your prayers."[3]

Over the next month, John Paul began to set out his hopes for his papacy and be responsive to the needs of the world. He refrained from using the royal *We* to refer to himself in papal communications. He did away with the papal tiara and portable throne. He publicly prayed for the tense negotiations between Israel and Egypt at Camp David in early September of 1978 and even intervened in tensions between Argentina and Chile. Most importantly for those interested in Catholic social teaching, John Paul set out a clear plan for his papacy, which signaled how he looked to carry on the mission of the Church: to continue the renewal of the Vatican Council II; to encourage Catholics to preach the Gospel; to complete Paul VI's revision of the Code of Canon Law; to promote unity and foster dialogue across religions; and to build global peace and justice.

Sadly, John Paul would not see the completion of his plan. Having been treated for a cardiac condition since his days as patriarch of Venice, he complained of chest pains on the evening of September 28, 1978. The next morning, he passed away, likely from a heart attack, and was laid to rest in St. Peter's Basilica the next week. His cause for canonization was opened in 1990 and a miracle in 2011 was investigated under then-Archbishop of Buenos Aires Jorge Mario Bergoglio. The same man, as Pope Francis, declared John Paul I venerable in 2017 and later beatified him in 2022. Pope Francis reminded the crowd of John Paul's beloved smile, encouraging the whole Church to live in the same way: "in the joy of the Gospel, without compromises, loving to the very end."[4]

WORDS TO ENLIGHTEN AND GUIDE

Address to the Diplomatic Corps,
August 31, 1978

The excerpt below comes from John Paul I's Address to the Diplomatic Corps at the Vatican. The Diplomatic Corps is made up of an ambassadorial staff from countries who have official relations with the Holy See. In the address, John Paul speaks of his deep desire to continue the diplomatic work of Paul VI despite his own lack of experience and of the task of working together to build peace.

> But [the Church's] activity, at the service of the international community, is . . . a matter of contributing . . . to forming consciences . . . regarding the fundamental principles that guarantee authentic civilization and real brotherhood between peoples. These principles are: respect for one's neighbour, for his life and for his dignity, care for his spiritual and social progress, patience and the desire for reconciliation in the fragile building up of peace.

Reflect and Pray

What word or phrase strikes you most from the excerpt above? What do you think God might be saying to you through that word or phrase? Take a few moments to respond to the Spirit's prompting and then silently rest in God's presence.

Urbi et Orbi Radio Message, August 27, 1978

A papal Urbi et Orbi message is an address and blessing to the whole world. It is usually given on Christmas, Easter, and the election of a new pope. When a pope gives an Urbi et Orbi, he is speaking to the entire Church. The excerpt below comes from John Paul I's only Urbi et Orbi message, in which he outlines how he hopes to lead the Church and his desires for not only Christians but all people in the world.

> In that light, we place . . . all of our physical and spiritual strength at the service of the universal mission of the Church. . . . In other words we will be at the service of truth, of justice, of peace, of harmony, of collaboration within nations as well as rapport among peoples. We call especially on the children of the Church to understand better their responsibility: "You are the salt of the earth, you are the light of the world" (Mt 5:13).

Reflect and Pray

Write down the characteristics and benefits of salt and light. How can the Church and each of us individually exemplify those characteristics in the world today? Bring your reflections, concerns, and hopes to Jesus in prayer.

Homily on Taking Possession of the Chair of the Bishop of Rome, September 23, 1978

After the Mass that installs the new pope as the successor of Peter, every pontiff celebrates a Mass at the Basilica of St. John Lateran in Rome in which the new pope officially takes up his seat as bishop of the Diocese of Rome. At this Mass, the new pope addresses the people of Rome as their new bishop and speaks on his hopes for the local community. Even in this moment, John Paul I demonstrates his humility and care for the poor, asking Romans to draw near to all those in need.

> Rome will be a true Christian community if God is honoured by you not merely with a multitude of the faithful in the churches, not merely with private life that is lived morally, but also with love for the poor. These, the Roman deacon Lawrence said, are the true treasures of the Church. They must be helped, however, by those who can, to have more and to be more, without becoming humiliated and offended by ostentatious riches, by money squandered on futile things and not invested—in so far as is possible—in enterprises of advantage to all.

Reflect and Pray

Read or listen to James 2:1–18. How does John Paul draw from this scripture passage? How does he expand upon it? What do your reflections reveal about who God is and how God loves?

General Audience, September 6, 1978

Every Wednesday in the modern era, popes have used general audiences to receive pilgrims and visitors to the Vatican and instruct on the faith. John Paul I continued the tradition of Paul VI in focusing his catechesis on the contemporary concerns and needs of the faithful. In his first audience on September 6, 1978, John Paul discusses what it means to follow the commandments in our daily lives.

> There are usually two virtues to observe: justice and charity. But charity is the soul of justice. We must love our neighbour, the Lord recommended it so much. I always recommend not only great acts of charity, but little ones.

Reflect and Pray

John Paul reminds us that, while justice requires addressing large systems and structures, it also requires small acts of charity. In prayer, identify small ways you can practice selfless giving throughout this week and commit to trying at least one of them.

General Audience, September 20, 1978

In his third general audience, John Paul I discusses the virtue of hope. He says that hope is necessary to all Christians in helping us sustain our work for human progress, inviting us to have an attitude of hope expressed in joy and cheerfulness. This attitude of hope helps us fight against pessimism and gives us courage in the face of so many social ills. Ultimately, John Paul says, our hope is not for this world alone but for eternal life with Jesus.

> I think that the Magisterium of the Church will never sufficiently insist in presenting and recommending the solution of the great problems of freedom, justice, peace, development; and Catholic laity will never fight sufficiently to solve these problems. . . . But if we pass from hope for the "world" to hope for individual souls, then we must speak also of "eternity."

Reflect and Pray

In working for justice, there's a temptation to focus only on the here and now. Choose one of the following scripture passages about eternity to pray with today: Isaiah 25:6-10, Deuteronomy 7:9–14, Luke 14:16–24, John 14:1–7, Revelation 21:1–7.

General Audience, September 27, 1978

This excerpt comes from John Paul I's last general audience, which took place the day before he died. In this audience, he discusses the third theological virtue: love. He opens the address with a simple prayer his mother taught him—an Act of Love that asks Jesus to help one grow in love for the Lord and for others. This excerpt below discusses the meaning of loving others as Christ commands.

> It is easy to love some persons; difficult to love others; we do not find them likeable, they have offended us and hurt us; only if I love God in earnest can I love them as [children] of God and because he asks me to. Jesus also established how to love one's neighbour: that is, not only with feeling, but with facts. This is the way, he said. I will ask you: I was hungry in the person of my humbler brothers, did you give me food? Did you visit me, when I was sick?

Reflect and Pray

Think of something that gives you joy. Let those good feelings well up inside of you. Now think of a difficult person and ask God to give that person the same joyful feelings. If it is hard, ask the Holy Spirit to soften your heart.

9.
POPE JOHN PAUL II

OCTOBER 16, 1978 – APRIL 2, 2005

✠ PAPAL MOTTO ✠

Totus tuus ~ Totally yours

St. John Paul II is undoubtedly one of the most important international figures of the twentieth century. The third-longest reigning pope, John Paul II served as the Successor of Peter for twenty-six years during an era of enormous political and technological change in which he brought the reforms of Vatican Council II to fruition. John Paul was both the first Slavic pope and the first non-Italian pope in over 450 years. He traveled more miles and encountered more people than any other pope in history. And when it comes to Catholic social teaching, no modern pope has contributed more writing to this topic than John Paul II.

Named for his father, Karol Wojtyła was born on May 18, 1920, in Poland during its brief period of national freedom from Soviet or German occupation in the twentieth century. Having lost his mother and only brother as a child, Wojtyła was brought up mainly by his father, an ardent Catholic. Karol Wojtyła was an intelligent, personable, and athletic young man who loved the arts as well as his faith. He enrolled in undergraduate studies in Kraków with great academic success until his studies were interrupted by the German invasion of Poland in 1939. After attempting to flee the country, Wojtyła and his father returned to Kraków where Wojtyła clandestinely continued his studies at night after working at a local factory during the day—making him the only modern pope to have worked as a laborer.

During this time, he also participated in a secret movement against the racial codes of the Nazi occupiers, promoting Polish drama and the arts. After the loss of his father in 1941, he entered the underground seminary. Wojtyła was ordained in 1946 and completed the first of his doctoral degrees in theology following his ordination. He eventually completed a second doctorate in philosophy and became a college professor at the University of Lübeck.

At the university, Wojtyła ministered to the young people in defiance of the Soviet regime. His success at the university both academically and pastorally brought him to the attention of Church hierarchy and eventually led to his ordination as auxiliary bishop of Krakow by Paul VI in 1958. As bishop, he attended Vatican Council II where his contributions were so exemplary that he was asked to collaborate with the writers of the Pastoral Constitution, *Gaudium et Spes*, and was made archbishop of Kraków in 1963. Only four years later, Wojtyła received the cardinal's pallium.

Over the next decade as archbishop of Kraków, Wojtyła fought against the oppressive Soviet rule of Poland. He encouraged the burgeoning Solidarity movement in Poland and frequently pushed for religious services to be held publicly as well as churches to be built in newly founded suburban communities. Denied access to the media and a traditional pulpit, Wojtyła and his fellow bishops organized large gatherings and grassroots movements, through which he developed his charismatic public speaking style.

In 1978, Wojtyła was elected pope and, in honor of his predecessor, chose the name John Paul II, signaling his commitment to continue the reforms of the Vatican Council II. Calling on the Church to "open wide the doors for Christ" at his installation Mass,[1] John Paul set about working for religious freedom, national independence, and human rights all over the world. He was the youngest pope in over a century, and his energy and engagement with the faithful quickly made him popular. His charismatic preaching, involvement with pressing global matters, and worldwide travel simultaneously launched him into the international sphere of influence.

On May 13, 1981, John Paul was shot in an attempted assassination during an audience in St. Peter's Square.

Attributing his survival to the intercession of the Blessed Mother, he forgave his attacker and maintained a lifelong friendship with the man. This attempt on his life did not deter the pope from his mission to preach the Gospel; John Paul spent the next twenty years traveling the world.

He frequently met with Jewish and Muslim leaders to develop interfaith dialogue and unity between the Abrahamic religions. He became the first pope to visit and pray at the Great Mosque of Mecca and to pray at the Wailing Wall, the only remaining wall of the Jerusalem Temple. He also issued formal apologies on behalf of the Church for its participation in the evils of anti-Semitism, colonialism, the slave trade, the Crusades, and other such dark moments in history. John Paul wrote extensively, including papal documents, books, letters, and speeches. Significantly, when it comes to doctrine, John Paul commissioned and promulgated a new version of the *Catechism of the Catholic Church*, the first in four centuries.

John Paul was keenly aware of the need for the Church to be a moral leader on social issues. In his encyclicals and exhortations, he discussed many of the same issues as his predecessors, such as the right of laborers and the need for peace. However, he also addressed new and pressing topics, such as racism, the growing need for the ethical practice of science and medicine, the rights of women, the increasing secularization of society, and—most importantly—the dignity and inviolability of human life from conception to natural death.

After a long decline due to Parkinson's disease, John Paul II died on April 2, 2005, mourned by millions around the world. He was beatified in 2011 by his friend and successor Pope Benedict XVI and canonized by Pope Francis in 2014. His legacy has been criticized by some due to indications that he initially overlooked much of the Church's sexual abuse scandals of the 2000s and other concerns regarding his approach to Church governance. These critiques serve as a reminder that even canonized saints can have deeply human shortcomings. Every person needs the mercy and grace of Jesus, who alone is perfect. We can also be encouraged that, as we struggle and strive for holiness, every saint struggled too. By God's grace, Pope John Paul II helped many people hear the Good News of Jesus and, sinful and still striving, we are able to do the same.

WORDS TO ENLIGHTEN AND GUIDE

Laborem Exercens ~ *On Human Work*, September 14, 1981

Laborem Exercens, 9

Written to honor the ninetieth anniversary of *Rerum Novarum*, the encyclical *Laborem Exercens* (*On Human Work*) was completed in 1981. A trained philosopher, John Paul incorporates his academic discipline in all of his writings. Here, he discusses the human being as a *subject*, that is, a rational being with free will who can create and express themselves through their actions. Humans engage in work *as* subjects—expressing their identity, creativity, and free will in all of their work.

> [Work] is not only good in the sense that it is useful or something to enjoy; it is also good as being something worthy, that is to say, something that corresponds to [human] dignity, that expresses this dignity and increases it. . . . Work is a good thing for man—a good thing for his humanity—because through work man *not only transforms nature*, adapting it to his own needs, but he also achieves *fulfilment* as a human being and indeed, in a sense, becomes "more a human being."

Reflect and Pray

In conversation with the Lord, reflect on the different types of work in your life (even if you aren't earning income for them). Tell God which are fulfilling, which are draining, and what you hope for your life at this moment in time.

Sollicitudo Rei Socialis ~ *On Social Concerns*, December 30, 1987

Sollicitudo Rei Socialis, 39

Sollicitudo Rei Socialis, promulgated in 1987, was written on the twentieth anniversary of *Populorum Progressio*. Drawing inspiration from Paul VI's encyclical, *Sollicitudo Rei Socialis* is meant to address new matters that relate to and impact human progress. As he discusses the specific challenges of contemporary issues, John Paul grounds his discourse in the virtue of solidarity.

> Solidarity helps us to see the "other"—whether a person, people or nation—not just as some kind of instrument, with a work capacity and physical strength to be exploited at low cost and then discarded when no longer useful, but as our "neighbor," a "helper" (cf. Gen 2:18–20), to be made a sharer, on a par with ourselves, in the banquet of life to which all are equally invited by God.

Reflect and Pray

Pray with God's commands to the Israelites in Deuteronomy 24:17–22. Why do you think God asked the Israelites to remember their time in Egypt as an act of solidarity with those in need? What does this teach us about who God is?

Reconciliatio et Paenitentia ~ *Reconciliation and Penance*, December 2, 1984

Reconciliatio et Paenitentia, 16

In *Sollicitudo Rei Socialis*, John Paul introduces the concept of *structures of sin*, or social realities that exist because of the sinful actions of many individuals and require social justice to repair. He discusses this idea further in his apostolic exhortation *Reconciliatio et Paenitentia* as a catechesis on sin, reconciliation, and penance. John Paul makes it clear that while the effects of sin have social impacts, those effects do not eliminate our own culpability.

> Whenever the Church speaks of situations of sin or when she condemns as social sins certain situations or the collective behavior of certain social groups, big or small . . . she knows and she proclaims that such cases of social sin are the result of the accumulation and concentration of many personal sins. It is a case of the very personal sins of those who cause or support evil or who exploit it; of those who are in a position to avoid, eliminate or at least limit certain social evils but who fail to do so . . . in the supposed impossibility of changing the world. . . . The real responsibility, then, lies with individuals.

Reflect and Pray

Take a moment to reflect on the wider impact of your own sins. Then, breathing deeply, repeat this ancient prayer from the Eastern Church: *Lord Jesus Christ, Son of God, have mercy on me, a sinner.*

Centesimus Annus ~ *On the Hundredth Anniversary of* Rerum Novarum, May 1, 1991

Centesimus Annus, 39

John Paul II revisits his reflections on *Rerum Novarum* in his 1991 encyclical *Centesimus Annus* (*On the Hundredth Anniversary of* Rerum Novarum). In honor of the centennial anniversary of Leo XIII's great encyclical, John Paul reflects on the global economy after the fall of the Soviet Union and a time of commerce driven by Western free market economics. He once again calls for human dignity and community to be put at the center of modern progress.

> The economy in fact is only one aspect and one dimension of the whole of human activity. If economic life is absolutized, if the production and consumption of goods become the centre of social life and society's only value, not subject to any other value, the reason is to be found not so much in the economic system itself as in the fact that the entire socio-cultural system, by ignoring the ethical and religious dimension, has been weakened, and ends by limiting itself to the production of goods and services alone.

Reflect and Pray

Write down or reflect on your answer to the following question: What would the world look like if the economy were at the service of social life? Once answered, sit silently and pay attention to what thoughts and feelings the Holy Spirit brings forth in you.

Centesimus Annus, 58

John Paul sees *Centesimus Annus* as a "look to the future" (*Centesimus Annus*, 3) amid the new challenges of the imminent twenty-first century. He commends the many people who have studied the Church's social teaching over the years, but reminds the whole Church that Catholic social teaching is not "a theory, but above all else a basis and a motivation for action" (*Centesimus Annus*, 57). Love must be made concrete.

> Love for others . . . is made concrete in the *promotion of justice*. Justice will never be fully attained unless people see . . . an opportunity for showing kindness and a chance for greater enrichment. Only such an awareness can give the courage needed to face the risk and the change involved in every authentic attempt to come to the aid of another. It is not merely a matter of "giving from one's surplus." . . . It requires above all a change of lifestyles, of models of production and consumption, and of the established structures of power which today govern societies.

Reflect and Pray

Love in action requires the courage to change, to live differently than our culture says we should. We receive the Spirit's gift of courage in the Sacrament of Confirmation. Ask the Spirit to draw out that gift in you today.

Evangelium Vitae ~ The Gospel of Life, March 25, 1995

Evangelium Vitae, 2

This encyclical was written in 1995 in response to the increasing prevalence of abortion, reproductive technologies, and euthanasia. John Paul presents the stark contrast between the culture of death, which discards those who are no longer useful, and the culture of life, which values human life from conception to natural death. For John Paul, the gospel of life is realized in self-gift, which has its most profound expression in the death and resurrection of Jesus.

> The Church knows that this Gospel of life . . . has a profound and persuasive echo in the heart of every person—believer and non-believer alike. . . . Even in the midst of difficulties and uncertainties, every person sincerely open to truth and goodness can . . . recognize . . . the sacred value of human life from its very beginning until its end, and can affirm the right of every human being to have this primary good respected to the highest degree. Upon the recognition of this right, every human community and the political community itself are founded.

Reflect and Pray

Make a list of five small things you are grateful for this week—a comfortable seat, a favorite song, a hearty laugh. Thank God for the gift of life and the good things in it.

10. POPE BENEDICT XVI

APRIL 18, 2005 – FEBRUARY 28, 2013

✠ PAPAL MOTTO ✠

Cooperatores veritatis ~
Cooperators of the truth

Reserved, calm, and intelligent, Pope Benedict XVI was one of the most influential Catholic theologians of the twentieth century, even before he was elected pope. He wrote dozens of books on theology, acted as a theological contributor for many of the key documents of Vatican Council II, and oversaw the 1992 revision of the *Catechism of the Catholic Church*. To those who knew him personally, though, Benedict was known for his large library, love of Mozart, decisiveness, and quiet kindness. When he made the historic decision to resign from the papacy in 2013, he brought his library to his new apartments, where he offered support and encouragement to Pope Francis, his successor.

Joseph Ratzinger was born in Germany on April 16, 1927. His parents, Joseph Ratzinger Sr., a police officer, and Maria Ratzinger (née Peintner), were devout Catholics who encouraged their three children to keep the faith even as the Nazi Party rose to power. The family deeply resented the Nazis and Ratzinger would recall in his memoirs seeing a parish priest beaten by local Nazi enforcers just before celebrating the Mass. At age fourteen, like all boys of that age, Ratzinger was forced to join the Hitler Youth but refused to attend meetings. He had a cousin of the same age with Down syndrome who was seized and murdered by the Nazis. Young Ratzinger was in seminary in 1943 when drafted into the auxiliary antiaircraft service. Later he trained in the German infantry. During his time in uniform, Ratzinger was imprisoned in US prisoner-of-war camps. As the Allied front drew close to his post in 1945, Ratzinger deserted and went back home. The horrors of World War II left deep wounds for the Ratzinger family, as for all of Europe.

After the war, Joseph Ratzinger began university studies, completing his degree in 1951. He was ordained to the priesthood on the same day as his brother, Georg. Two years later, Ratzinger received a doctoral degree in theology and began his first position as a university professor, a role he would hold for the majority of his life. Over the next decades he became one of the most esteemed Catholic theologians in the world, receiving multiple honorary degrees as well as acting as a theological adviser for Vatican Council II. In 1977, Pope Paul VI appointed him cardinal and archbishop of Munich and Freising, where he spent the next five years leading the archdiocese.

In 1981, Pope John Paul II, a friend and fellow academic, appointed Ratzinger as the head of the Congregation for the Doctrine of the Faith, which is known today as the Dicastery for the Doctrine of the Faith. In this role, Ratzinger was meticulous and somewhat stringent in his oversight, swiftly challenging theological movements that he felt strayed too far from the Church's teaching. Yet, his role in this congregation, including his work on the new *Catechism* and as president of both the Pontifical Biblical Commission and the International Theological Commission, was also fruitful and foundational for the Church. More importantly, however, it was Ratzinger who, in 2001, realized the scope of the sexual abuse scandal within the Church when he discovered that bishops were simply moving offending clergy from parish to parish. Ratzinger assumed responsibility for processing offense cases and continued these efforts during his papacy, leading to sanctions or removal for more than 3,300 clergy.

When John Paul II passed away in 2005, the conclave to choose his successor was fast and decisive. They chose Ratzinger to lead the Church in twenty-four hours. The new Pope Benedict XVI, only two years from retiring from the College of Cardinals during the conclave, later said that his election to the papacy felt like "a guillotine" coming down on him.[1] The oldest elected pope since the eighteenth century, Benedict took up the Chair of Peter in a world wildly different from what John Paul had inherited in 1978. Globalization was rapidly increasing with the rise of the internet. Religious violence was on the rise, profoundly linked to global terrorism, and created deep divisions between the Abrahamic religions. Yet Benedict did not shy away from this reality. Instead, he tried to meet it with attempts to heal the internal and external life of the Church—often with mixed success.

Like John Paul II, Benedict emphasized dialogue and friendship with the Jewish and Muslim people. He also signaled his openness to restoring diplomatic relations with China, which had ended in 1951 during its communist revolution. He updated the Church's legal codes, required the bishops' conferences in each country to come up with new policies for preventing abuse, wept and prayed with survivors of clergy sexual abuse, and began a path to financial transparency in the Vatican. While not always successful in his attempts at reconciliation or public relations, Benedict wanted healing and a return to Christian ethics around the world.

Although Benedict was a prolific writer and authored over sixty books, he wrote relatively few encyclicals and apostolic letters compared to his predecessors. However, his three encyclicals were particularly profound reflections on the message of the Gospel for the twenty-first century. In each of his apostolic writings Benedict calls the Church to keep Jesus at the center of its life and doctrine. His approach to the Church's Tradition, especially its social teaching, is best summarized in his first encyclical, *Deus Caritas Est*. He writes, "We have come to believe in God's love: in these words, the Christian can express the fundamental decision of his life. Being Christian is not the result of an ethical choice or a lofty idea, but the encounter with an event, a person, which gives life a new horizon and a decisive direction" (*Deus Caritas Est*, 1).

In 2013, Benedict announced that he would be stepping down from the papacy. As the first pope in six hundred years to resign from the Chair of Peter, Benedict set a modern precedent of discernment, opening the door to a similar choice for future popes. On the appointed day of his resignation and the beginning of the conclave, Benedict removed himself from the Vatican for a few months until the newly elected Pope Francis was fully installed as his successor. Benedict spent the rest of his life in quiet retirement in a Vatican apartment, visiting with friends and family and acting as a support for Pope Francis. He passed away on December 31, 2022, and is buried in St. Peter's Basilica. He is remembered as an intellectual giant of our time and a pope who always strove to choose the good of the Church.

WORDS TO ENLIGHTEN AND GUIDE

Deus Caritas Est ~ *God Is Love*, December 25, 2005

Deus Caritas Est, 28b

Deus Caritas Est (*God Is Love*) was Benedict XVI's first encyclical, promulgated in 2005. In a world anxious from global terrorism and growing religious violence, Benedict felt the message that God is love was "both timely and significant" (*Deus Caritas Est*, 1). In this excerpt, Benedict expands on the biblical truth that the greatest of all virtues is love (1 Cor 13:13).

> Love—*caritas*—will always prove necessary, even in the most just society. There is no ordering of the State so just that it can eliminate the need for a service of love. . . . There will always be suffering which cries out for consolation and help. There will always be loneliness. There will always be situations of material need where help in the form of concrete love of neighbor is indispensable. The State which would provide everything, absorbing everything into itself, would ultimately become a mere bureaucracy incapable of guaranteeing the very thing which the suffering person—every person—needs: namely, loving personal concern.

Reflect and Pray

Human life will never be perfect on this earth. But the love we share with others will echo into eternity. How do you need to be loved and cared for this week? Who in your life needs loving concern? Bring your reflections to prayer.

Caritas in Veritate ~ *Charity in Truth*, June 29, 2009

Caritas in Veritate, 2

Benedict's second encyclical, *Caritas in Veritate* (*Charity in Truth*), was written in 2009 during the height of the global financial crisis. It was both a reflection on the fortieth anniversary of *Populorum Progressio* and an application of its principles to the worldwide recession. Benedict focuses on charity—a selfless love that goes above and beyond what is required—as the core message of Catholic social teaching in this document.

> Charity is at the heart of the Church's social doctrine. Every responsibility and every commitment spelt out by that doctrine is derived from charity which, according to the teaching of Jesus, is the synthesis of the entire Law (cf. Mt 22:36–40). It gives real substance to the personal relationship with God and with neighbour; it is the principle not only of micro-relationships (with friends, with family members or within small groups) but also of macro-relationships (social, economic and political ones).

Reflect and Pray

What do you think it means to have charity in macro-relationships as Benedict describes above? How can you bring a selfless heart to your social, economic, and political lives? Bring your reflections to prayer.

Caritas in Veritate, 6

Benedict meditates on the gratuitousness of God's love in *Caritas in Veritate*—a love that gives lavishly and often illogically, with no prerequisites or expectations of return. He says that Christians must have a posture of gratuitousness in our personal relationships and in our global community. However, that gratuitousness must always include justice.

> Charity goes beyond justice, because to love is to give, to offer what is "mine" to the other; but it never lacks justice, which prompts us to give the other what is "his", what is due to him by reason of his being or his acting. I cannot "give" what is mine to the other, without first giving him what pertains to him in justice. If we love others with charity, then first of all we are just towards them.

Reflect and Pray

Pray with Philippians 2:1–11. Notice the word, phrase, or image that stands out to you most What might God be saying to you about justice and charity? How would you respond to the Lord? Take a moment to rest in God's presence.

Caritas in Veritate, 7

A central theme of *Caritas in Veritate* is how economic systems exist in service to the common good; human development is both communal and individual. Therefore, economies must serve both the good of the individual and the common good. This also means that charitable love, which goes beyond justice alone, similarly takes both a communal and individual form.

> To love someone is to desire that person's good and to take effective steps to secure it. Besides the good of the individual, there is a good that is linked to living in society: the common good. . . . It is a good that is sought not for its own sake, but for the people who belong to the social community and who can only really and effectively pursue their good within it. . . . The more we strive to secure a common good corresponding to the real needs of our neighbours, the more effectively we love them.

Reflect and Pray

Pray for the common good. Identify a person or group of people from your loved ones, local community, nation, and greater world. Intercede for their needs and ask God to bring about their flourishing.

Sacramentum Caritatis ~ *The Sacrament of Charity*, February 22, 2007

Sacramentum Caritatis, 88

Sacramentum Caritatis (*The Sacrament of Charity*) is a 2007 apostolic exhortation that followed the Synod of Bishops on the Eucharist. In addition to summarizing the synod's conclusions, Pope Benedict states that he wants this exhortation to be read alongside *Deus Caritas Est* as a meditation on the Eucharist and its relationship to Christian love (*Sacramentum Caritatis*, 5).

> Our communities, when they celebrate the Eucharist, must become ever more conscious that the sacrifice of Christ is for all, and that the Eucharist thus compels all who believe in him to become "bread that is broken" for others, and to work for the building of a more just and fraternal world. . . . Each of us is truly called, together with Jesus, to be bread broken for the life of the world.

Reflect and Pray

In what ways do you experience the love of Christ in the Eucharist? What do you hear for your life in Pope Benedict XVI's teaching that we are all called, by our participation in the Eucharistic mystery, to become "bread broken for the life of the world"? How do you try to do this?

Sacramentum Caritatis, 89

In *Sacramentum Caritatis*, Benedict XVI says that the Mass is the "school of the Eucharist" that forms the laity for political and social responsibilities (*Sacramentum Caritatis*, 91). He asks the faithful to consider the implications of the "mystery of liberation that constantly and insistently challenges us" in imitating this sacrament (*Sacramentum Caritatis*, 89). Drawing closer to the heart of Christ, we are transformed to increase in love for all those he loves.

> The union with Christ brought about by the Eucharist also brings a newness to our social relations. . . . The relationship between the eucharistic mystery and social commitment must be made explicit. The Eucharist is the sacrament of communion between brothers and sisters who allow themselves to be reconciled in Christ. . . . The recognition of this fact leads to a determination to transform unjust structures and to restore respect for the dignity of all. . . . Through the concrete fulfilment of this responsibility, the Eucharist becomes in life what it signifies in its celebration.

Reflect and Pray

This week at Mass, try to listen attentively to the Prayer after Communion (or read it in a missal, or online!). This short prayer often connects our Communion to our mission in the world. Bring a theme or phrase from that prayer into your personal prayer this week. For right now, reflect on how you allow the Eucharist to inform and direct your involvement in the social sphere, which the Church calls us to be aimed at restoring the dignity due to all people. Ask the Holy Spirit to show you how to strengthen this work in you.

11.
POPE FRANCIS

MARCH 13, 2013 – APRIL 21, 2025

✱ PAPAL MOTTO ✱

Miserando atque eligendo ~

By having mercy and by choosing

Francis was widely seen as a pope of the people. Known for his humility, compassion, and commitment to the poor and marginalized, Francis spent much of his papacy urging the faithful to be missionary disciples who went out of their homes and churches to share the love of Jesus. He advocated tirelessly for peace in the world, as well as protection of the Earth through environmental stewardship and intercultural exchange. Francis's pontificate might be called an incarnated catechesis on Catholic social teaching as he taught the Church and the world how to truly see and accompany the poor, by whom he meant all in the world on the margins of societies.

Those who knew Jorge Mario Bergoglio in Buenos Aires were likely expecting such a course of action from him. Born to Italian immigrants in Argentina on December 17, 1936, Bergoglio was one of five children in his devout Catholic family. As a young man, Bergoglio completed training as a chemical technician before discerning a vocation to join the Society of Jesus in 1958. His mother was initially opposed to his entering the seminary but later encouraged him to follow his path toward priesthood. He was ordained in 1969 and became the Jesuit provincial of Argentina in 1973. In 1980, he became seminary rector and remained there until 1986 when he completed his doctorate of theology in Germany.

Bergoglio was a popular priest known for his very personable pastoral style and his nearness to the people. When in 1992 the archbishop of Buenos Aires requested that Bergoglio become one of his auxiliary bishops, Pope John Paul II appointed Bergoglio to the archdiocese. In 1998, Bergoglio assumed that office and was well-respected throughout Argentina and Latin America for his compassion and humility. It was common knowledge that he eschewed the archbishop's residence, preferring a small apartment in the city center, and used public transportation to be closer to his fellow city dwellers and the flock whom he served.

Pope John Paul II named Bergoglio a cardinal in 2001, and that same year, Bergoglio served in key roles during the Synod on Episcopal Ministry, introducing the theme and discussions of the synod as well as overseeing the preparation of the final document. At the synod he spoke about "the prophetic mission of the bishop," which prefigured many of the themes of his papacy. It reflected much of the missionary project he had undertaken in the Archdiocese of Buenos Aires, a project that invited the diocese to engage in intentional community, lay leadership, evangelization, and service to the poor and infirm. In 2005, Bergoglio was also elected president of the Episcopal Conference of Argentina and served in this role until 2011.

When Benedict XVI resigned in 2013, Bergoglio was elected as pope within forty-eight hours. He chose the name Francis to honor St. Francis of Assisi and the Jesuit St. Francis Xavier, both missionaries and preachers. The first pope from the Jesuit order and the Americas, Francis met a world hungry for love with a joyful and tender embrace. He continued the tradition of his predecessors in traveling the world engaging with other cultures and meeting with both religious and political leaders to advocate for peace, reconciliation, and human dignity.

Francis also continued the practice of publicly acknowledging the Church's participation in historically devasting wrongs. In 2022, he took a penitential pilgrimage to Canada to apologize for the Church's part in the Canadian Indian boarding school system that attempted to forcibly assimilate Indigenous children into Anglo culture through widespread neglect and abuse. He became the first pope to visit the Arabian Peninsula where he met with the grand imam of the University of Cairo, and together they issued a joint statement on peace. Francis also initiated further reforms of the Vatican's finances and governance, including appointing women, both lay and religious, to key positions of power within Vatican City. One of his key contributions to the Church's social doctrine was the revision of a paragraph in the *Catechism of the Catholic Church* in 2018 to officially clarify that the death penalty is "inadmissible" because the conditions that once may have allowed for it no longer exist, and it "is an attack on the inviolability and dignity of the person" (*CCC*, 2267).

In 2024, Francis began to ease his travel and was often seen in a wheelchair during his public engagements. By 2025, he had been hospitalized multiple times and cut back significantly on his public duties. His last appearance to the faithful was on Easter Sunday that year, during which he gave the traditional Urbi et Orbi blessing. The next day, April 21, 2025, Francis passed away, leaving the Church forever changed by his leadership. His funeral was as simple as he was, including his choice to be buried in the Basilica of St. Mary Major, said to be his favorite church in Rome. Francis had a deep and consistent devotion to the Blessed Mother and his relatively small and simple burial niche is near his favorite icon of Mary, the Byzantine icon *Salus Populi Romani*, which Francis is said to have prayed at before and after every foreign trip of his papacy. His resting place in marked with a simple white burial stone bearing only his name, Franciscus.

WORDS TO ENLIGHTEN AND GUIDE

Laudato Si' ~ On Care for our Common Home, May 24, 2015

Laudato Si', 77

Francis's second encyclical draws on the work of John Paul II and Benedict XVI. It is the first social encyclical to primarily address care for creation and its connection to the Gospel. Francis invites the Church to consider creation's connection to God and its redemption through the Incarnation.

> The universe did not emerge as the result of arbitrary omnipotence, a show of force or a desire for self-assertion. Creation is of the order of love. God's love is the fundamental moving force in all created things. . . . Every creature is thus the object of the Father's tenderness, who gives it its place in the world. Even the fleeting life of the least of beings is the object of his love, and in its few seconds of existence, God enfolds it with his affection.

Reflect and Pray

Set aside time to spend in nature this week. Notice the beauty and detailed design of every part of your local environment. Consider these words of Pope Francis as you soak in the things of the Earth: "Even the fleeting life of the least of beings is the object of his love, and in its few seconds of existence, God enfolds it with his affection." Offer a prayer of gratitude for the gift of creation and for the Father's affection for all of it, including you.

Laudato Si', 93

Francis outlines how care of creation is intricately tied to the common good of all humanity, especially the poor. Drawing from Leo XIII, he asserts that not only do the goods of the earth belong to all people, but also "[the] natural environment is a collective good, the patrimony of all humanity and the responsibility of everyone" (*Laudato Si'*, 95).

> Whether believers or not, we are agreed today that the earth is essentially a shared inheritance, whose fruits are meant to benefit everyone. For believers, this becomes a question of fidelity to the Creator, since God created the world for everyone. Hence every ecological approach needs to incorporate a social perspective which takes into account the fundamental rights of the poor and the underprivileged.

Reflect and Pray

As an act of solidarity with the poor, try an "ecological fast" one day this week. Use as little energy and water and as few disposable products as possible. When finished, spend time reflecting and praying on the experience. Is there any part of the fast that you can build on or repeat on a regular basis? Did this experience shift your perspective on the goods of creation and our responsibility to use them for the benefit of all people?

Fratelli Tutti ~ *On Fraternity and Social Friendship,* October 3, 2020

Fratelli Tutti, 80

This third encyclical of Pope Francis focuses on the kinship of all people. He introduces the term *social friendship*, which he says is based on "a love capable of transcending borders" and is what "makes true universal openness possible." (*Fratelli Tutti*, 99). To give a fuller picture of social friendship, Francis unpacks the parable of the Good Samaritan.

> Jesus told the parable of the Good Samaritan in answer to the question: Who is my neighbor? The word "neighbor," in the society of Jesus's time, usually meant those nearest us. It was felt that help should be given primarily to those of one's own group and race. . . . Jesus . . . completely transforms this approach. He asks us not to decide who is close enough to be our neighbor, but rather that we ourselves become neighbors to all.

Reflect and Pray

Keeping Francis's words in mind, read the parable of the Good Samaritan (Lk 10:25–37). Who do you identify with in the story? Why? Bring your thoughts and reflections to prayer. Ask the Holy Spirit to help you see the ways this parable connects to your own life. Specifically, how do you strive to transcend borders or divisions in your everyday activities? Ask the Spirit for guidance in this.

Fratelli Tutti, 95

Fratelli Tutti was written at the height of the global COVID-19 pandemic. In many places around the world, people were socially isolated, and many experienced elevated levels of anxiety and fear. Acknowledging how the pandemic highlighted our global connectedness in both positive and negative ways, Pope Francis presents a hopeful model of how communion and social friendship are possible through Jesus Christ.

> Love also impels us towards universal communion. No one can mature or find fulfilment by withdrawing from others. By its very nature, love calls for growth in openness and the ability to accept others as part of a continuing adventure that makes every periphery converge in a greater sense of mutual belonging. As Jesus told us: "You are all brothers" (Mt 23:8).

Reflect and Pray

Identify the places in your life where you feel belonging and communion with others. What characteristics are present? How do you see God present? How can you apply the lessons learned from those experiences to welcome and connect with others, old and new, in your life? Following the example of Pope Francis, ask for the courage to reach out and build stronger connections with the people you encounter every day.

Fratelli Tutti, 215–216

Throughout his pontificate, Pope Francis expanded on Benedict XVI's understanding of Christianity as an encounter with Jesus. Francis invites the Church to a style of missionary discipleship that goes out to encounter others on the peripheries of society and help them to come to know Jesus. Here, he speaks of building a culture of encounter within the Church.

> I have frequently called for the growth of a culture of encounter capable of transcending our differences and divisions. . . . The word "culture" points to something deeply embedded within a people, its most cherished convictions and its way of life. . . . To speak of a "culture of encounter" means that we, as a people, should be passionate about meeting others, seeking points of contact, building bridges, planning a project that includes everyone. This becomes an aspiration and a style of life.

Reflect and Pray

What attitudes, postures, and perspectives are necessary to building a culture of encounter? What hopes, fears, and worries do those bring up in you? Bring these to prayer, opening yourself to the fullness of God's tender compassion and steadfast love.

Dilexit Nos ~ He Loves Us, October 24, 2024

Dilexit Nos, 214

Promulgated in 2024 near the end of Pope Francis's life, *Dilexet Nos* (*He Loves Us*) invites the Church into deeper love of Christ. Francis draws from mystics and doctors of the Church, pointing out that when we experience the love of God, we want to share it with others. Christians, he says, are called to bring that love to the world through both preaching the Good News of Jesus and serving their wider community.

> If we are concerned with helping others, this in no way means that we are turning away from Jesus. Rather, we are encountering him in another way. Whenever we try to help and care for another person, Jesus is at our side. We should never forget that, when he sent his disciples on mission, "the Lord worked with them" (Mk 16:20). He is always there, always at work, sharing our efforts to do good. In a mysterious way, his love becomes present through our service. He speaks to the world in a language that at times has no need of words.

Reflect and Pray

Breathing slowly and deeply, spend some time in silence, reflecting on Pope Francis's words and inviting the Holy Spirit to speak to your heart. After a few minutes, repeat this prayer several times and open your heart to receive its grace: *Lord Jesus, let me be your hands and feet.*

12.
POPE LEO XIV

MAY 8, 2025 – PRESENT

✠ PAPAL MOTTO ✠

In illo Uno unum ~

In the One, [we are] one

Within hours of learning Pope Leo XIV was born and raised in Chicago, the internet was awash with jokes about pizza, accents, and sports. While Pope Leo celebrates his Chicago roots, he is also a proud citizen of Peru, where he lived as a missionary and bishop for many years. The second pope from the Americas, following Francis, Leo is the first pope to belong to the Order of St. Augustine. He spent many years traveling the world as the Augustinian provincial. He can speak five languages and read seven. He is, like many popes before him, a man of the world. But those who know Pope Leo best describe him as a reflective, discerning person who cares deeply about the people of God.

Born Robert Francis Prevost on September 14, 1955, he is the youngest of three sons of Mildred Agnes (née Martínez) and Louis Marius Prevost. Educated at his parish's elementary school, Prevost was a bright child who went on to high school seminary with the Augustinians and eventually earned a degree in mathematics at Villanova University. Following university, he entered the novitiate with the Augustinians and professed solemn vows in 1981, being ordained the following year. In 1984, Prevost obtained his licentiate in canon law and was sent to the Augustinian mission in Peru in 1985. During that time, he defended his doctoral dissertation and, upon completion, was sent back to Chicago to serve as the province's vocations and mission director.

In 1987, Prevost was sent back to Peru where he spent more than a decade serving in the Archdiocese of Trujillo in both pastoral and administrative positions. In 1999, he was elected provincial prior of the Augustinian Chicago-based Midwest province and, two years later, prior general of the worldwide Augustinian order. After two terms as prior general, Prevost returned to Chicago in 2013 to serve as the formation director for the Augustinian novitiate until Pope Francis appointed him apostolic administrator of the Diocese of Chiclayo, Peru, in 2014. Prevost was ordained as an auxiliary bishop and then made the bishop of Chiclayo in 2015.

During the next five years, Pope Francis made Prevost a member of both the Dicastery for the Clergy and the Dicastery for Bishops. In 2023, Prevost was called to Rome after nearly a decade leading and serving the people of Chiclayo. In Rome, Prevost served as prefect of the Dicastery for Bishops and president of the Pontifical Commission for Latin America. He was made a cardinal by Pope Francis and, during the next two years in his role as prefect, Prevost oversaw the selection of bishops and worked closely with Pope Francis to meet and assist all bishops around the world. In his work, Prevost promoted missionary dialogue, synodality, and open engagement with social and technological changes affecting contemporary cultures around the world.

On May 8, 2025, on the second day of the conclave following the death of Pope Francis, Robert Francis Prevost was elected pope and took the name Leo XIV in honor of Pope Leo XIII, signaling to the world that he would follow Leo XIII's deep concern and commitment to the social teachings of the Church. Specifically, Pope Leo XIV noted early in his papacy the need of the Church to address growing threats to human dignity brought about by AI development, and the need for the Church to once again take up the rights of workers in a this new technological age.

The first months of Leo's papacy reflected his intent to continue the legacy of Pope Francis. He asked the cardinals to renew their commitment to the teachings of the Vatican Council II and to Francis's vision of evangelization as laid out in his apostolic exhortation *Evangelii Gaudium*. Leo has already shown his care for migrants, affirmed the importance of human life and creativity, spoken out against violence, and invited the Church to continue to build a culture of encounter. As the Church looks to her future under the leadership of a new pontiff, we can expect that future to be one that continues the long tradition of social engagement with the peoples and nations of the world, proclaiming the Gospel message of salvation in Christ Jesus. Leo XIV has reminded us that just as Leo XIII set out to have the Church lead the world toward a lasting peace, which requires the work of social justice, he also heralded the importance of addressing the "new things" that were reshaping the world. Pope Leo XIV is following a similar path, challenging all of us to bring the timeless proclamation of the Good News of Jesus Christ to a world full "of new things."

WORDS TO ENLIGHTEN AND GUIDE

Address to Members of the International Inter-Parliamentary Union, June 21, 2025

The Inter-Parliamentary Union (IPU) is an international organization of 181 of the 190 national parliaments. It connects members of parliaments from around the world to work together for democracy, human rights, and the promotion of the common good. In June 2025, about six weeks after Pope Leo's election, members of the IPU gathered at the Vatican for an audience with the new pope. He spoke about their shared goals and the importance of upholding human rights.

> Our personal life has greater value than any algorithm, and social relationships require spaces for development that far transcend the limited patterns that any soulless machine can pre-package. Let us not forget that, while able to store millions of data points and answer many questions in a matter of seconds, artificial intelligence remains equipped with a "static memory" [incomparable to] human beings. Our memory, on the other hand, is creative, dynamic, generative, capable of uniting past, present and future in a lively and fruitful search for meaning, with all the ethical and existential implications that this entails.

Reflect and Pray

Consider the important people in your life, their unique stories, gifts, and talents. Consider your own story. How has God shaped all of these lives? What would be missing in the world without them? Offer a prayer of thanksgiving for each person (yourself included!), and pray for their needs.

Message for the Ninth World Day of the Poor, June 13, 2025

Established by Pope Francis in 2017, the World Day of the Poor is an annual observance on the Thirty-Third Sunday of Ordinary Time. Francis established the observance to remind the Church that "poverty is at the heart of the gospel."[1] Pope Leo issued his first message for the World Day of the Poor in June of 2025, reinforcing the idea that, in the poor, one finds the face of Christ.

> The poor are not a distraction for the Church, but our beloved brothers and sisters, for by their lives, their words and their wisdom, they put us in contact with the truth of the Gospel. . . . [The] poor are at the heart of all our pastoral activity. This is true not only of the Church's charitable work, but also of the message that she celebrates and proclaims. God took on their poverty in order to enrich us through their voices, their stories and their faces. Every form of poverty, without exception, calls us to experience the Gospel concretely and to offer effective signs of hope.

Reflect and Pray

It is far too easy to view those in need as objects of one's service and forget that they have wisdom and gifts to offer too. Find a story from someone experiencing suffering, marginalization, or oppression—in person, online, or in a book—and allow the Holy Spirit to speak to you through their words.

Message for the Tenth World Day of Prayer for the Care of Creation, June 30, 2025

The World Day of Prayer for the Care of Creation was established by Pope Francis in 2015 as a day to "reaffirm [our] personal vocation to be stewards of creation, to thank God . . . and to implore his help for the protection of creation."[2] Pope Leo's first message for the September 1 celebration affirms Francis's call for environmental justice.

> Environmental justice—implicitly proclaimed by the prophets—can no longer be regarded as an abstract concept or a distant goal. It is an urgent need that involves much more than simply protecting the environment. For it is a matter of justice. . . . It is also a duty born of faith, since the universe reflects the face of Jesus Christ, in whom all things were created and redeemed. In a world where the most vulnerable . . . are the first to suffer the devastating effects of climate change, deforestation and pollution, care for creation becomes an expression of our faith and humanity.

Reflect and Pray

Pray with Proverbs 8:22–31. How does this call you to be a steward of creation? To environmental justice? Resolve to take one action this week to appreciate and care for the Earth.

General Audience, May 28, 2025

Like many of the modern popes, Leo has used his Wednesday general audiences to teach on the faith in a themed series. During this audience in late May, he continues a cycle of catechesis begun by Pope Francis during the Jubilee Year of Hope. The address centers on the parable of the Good Samaritan (Lk 10:25–31) and the importance of noticing others in order to be compassionate to them.

> Compassion is expressed through practical gestures. The Evangelist Luke ponders the actions of the [Good] Samaritan . . . a Samaritan approaches, because if you want to help someone, you cannot think of keeping your distance, you have to get involved, get dirty, perhaps be contaminated; he binds the wounds . . . he loads him onto his horse, taking on the burden, . . . willing to feel the weight of the other's pain; he takes him to an inn where he spends money . . . ; and he undertakes to return and eventually pay more, because the other is not a package to deliver, but someone to care for.

Reflect and Pray

Do an examination of conscience. Are you willing to get involved with people who are hurting? What do you do when things get hard or messy? Do you seek out people and communities who are different from you and your community? Or do you avoid the unknown, prioritizing comfort and safety? Ask God for the wisdom and courage of the Good Samaritan so that the next time you encounter someone in need, you will reach out with the love and compassion of Christ.

Homily at Mass for Corpus Christi, June 22, 2025

Pope Leo gave this homily on the feast of the Body and Blood of Christ (Corpus Christi). Preaching on the multiplication of the loaves and fishes (Lk 9:11–17), Leo reflects on both physical and spiritual hunger in our world. He asks us to consider the examples of Jesus from this story as a pattern for our own actions and Jesus himself as the answer to every hunger of the human heart.

> That is how Jesus satisfies the hunger of the crowd: he does what God does, and he teaches us to do the same. Today, . . . entire peoples are suffering more as a result of the greed of others than from their own hunger. . . . The amassing of wealth by a few is the sign of an arrogant indifference that produces pain and injustice. Rather than sharing, it squanders the fruits of the earth and human labour. . . . [The] Lord's example is a yardstick [for us]: we are called to share our bread, to multiply hope and to proclaim the coming of God's Kingdom.

Reflect and Pray

What does it mean to multiply hope in our world today? What habits might you develop or increase to proclaim with your actions and attitudes the full flowering of God's kingdom? How can these draw you closer to God? Offer your reflections to the Lord in prayer.

Homily at Mass for Pentecost, June 8, 2025

Pentecost is called the birthday of the Church, the day when the Spirit descended and emboldened the apostles to leave the upper room. In his homily on Pentecost, Pope Leo expounds on the words of Benedict XVI, who noted that where the Spirit is at work, the Spirit opens borders.[3] Here, Leo discusses the apostles preaching to the crowds in Acts 2:1–13.

> Finally, the Spirit also opens borders between peoples. At Pentecost, the Apostles spoke the languages of those they met, and the confusion of Babel was finally resolved by the harmony brought about by the Spirit. Whenever God's "breath" unites our hearts and makes us view others as our brothers and sisters, differences no longer become an occasion for division and conflict but rather a shared patrimony from which we can all draw, and which sets us all on journey together, in fraternity.

Reflect and Pray

True communion is only possible by God's grace. Transformation is not only a human activity but the work of the Holy Spirit. Ask the Holy Spirit to continue the good work God has begun in your heart (Phil 1:6) and to renew the face of the earth (Ps 104:30).

NOTES

Introduction by Katie Prejean McGrady

1. Pope Leo XIV, "Address of His Holiness Pope Leo XIV to the College of Cardinals," The Holy See, May 10, 2025, www.vatican.va/content/leo-xiv/en/speeches/2025/may/documents/20250510-collegio-cardinalizio.html.

2. Pope Leo XIV, "First Blessing "Urbi et Orbi" of His Holiness Pope Leo XIV," The Holy See, May 8, 2025, www.vatican.va/content/leo-xiv/en/messages/urbi/documents/20250508-prima-benedizione-urbietorbi.html.

2. Pope Pius X

1. "Saint Pius X," Saint of the Day August 21, Franciscan Media, accessed July 9, 2025, www.franciscanmedia.org/saint-of-the-day/saint-pius-x/.

2. "Saint Pius X."

7. Pope Paul VI

1. "Pastoral Constitution on the Church in the Modern World Gaudium et Spes," The Holy See, December 7, 1965, www.vatican.va/archive/hist_councils/ii_vatican_council/documents/vat-ii_const_19651207_gaudium-et-spes_en.html.

8. Pope John Paul I

1. J. Peter Nixon, "Pope John Paul I, an alternative to the 'celebrity saint,'" US Catholic, August 31, 2022, uscatholic.org/articles/202208/pope-john-paul-i-an-alternative-to-the-celebrity-saint/.

2. Nixon, "Pope John Paul I."

3. Pope John Paul I, "Angelus," The Holy See, August 27, 1978, www.vatican.va/content/john-paul-i/en/angelus/documents/hf_jp-i_ang_27081978.html.

4. Pope Francis, "Holy Mass and Beatification of the Servant of God, Pope John Paul I Homily of his Holiness Pope Francis," The Holy See, September 4, 2022, www.vatican.va/content/francesco/en/homilies/2022/documents/20220904-omelia-beatificazione-gpi.html.

9. Pope John Paul II

1. Pope John Paul II, "Homily of His Holiness John Paul II for the Inauguration of His Pontificate," The Holy See, October 22, 1978, www.vatican.va/content/john-paul-ii/en/homilies/1978/documents/hf_jp-ii_hom_19781022_inizio-pontificato.html/.

10. Pope Benedict XVI

1. Nicole Winfield, "Benedict XVI, reluctant pope who chose to retire, dies at 95," Associated Press News, December 31, 2022, apnews.com/article/pope-benedict-xvi-a-life-remembered-ed6ddf20f696d84ffe0680e1ef0bab0f.

11. Pope Francis

1. "Biography of the Holy Father Francis," from *L'Osservatore Romano* 152, no. 61 (2014), The Holy See, www.vatican.va/content/francesco/en/biography/documents/papa-francesco-biografia-bergoglio.html.

12. Pope Leo XIV

1. "Pope Francis Morning Meditation in the Chapel of the *Domus Sanctae Marthae* Wealth and Poverty on Tuesday, 16 June 2015," from *L'Osservatore Romano*, no. 25 (June 19, 2015), The Holy See, www.vatican.va/content/francesco/en/cotidie/2015/documents/papa-francesco-cotidie_20150616_wealth-and-poverty.html.

2. Pope Francis, "Letter of His Holiness Pope Francis for the Establishment of the "World Day of Prayer for the Care of Creation" [1st September]," The Holy See, August 6, 2015, www.vatican.va/content/francesco/en/messages/cura-creato/documents/papa-francesco_20150806_lettera-giornata-cura-creato.html.

3. Benedict XVI, "Mass of His Priestly Ordination Homily of His Holiness Benedict XVI," The Holy See, May 15, 2005, www.vatican.va/content/benedict-xvi/en/homilies/2005/documents/hf_ben-xvi_hom_20050515_priestly-ordination.html.

BIBLIOGRAPHY

PROFILES

1. Pope Leo XIII

Aubert, Roger-François-Marie. "Leo XIII." *Britannica*, last updated June 5, 2025, www.britannica.com/biography/Leo-XIII.

Wells, Christopher. "Leo XIII's times and our own." Vatican News, May 14, 2025, www.vaticannews.va/en/church/news/2025-05/leo-xiii-s-times-and-our-own.html.

2. Pope Pius X

"Saint Pius X." Saint of the Day August 21, Franciscan Media, accessed July 9, 2025, www.franciscanmedia.org/saint-of-the-day/saint-pius-x/.

The Editors of Encyclopaedia Britannica. "St. Pius X." *Britannica*, last updated May 29, 2025, www.britannica.com/biography/Saint-Pius-X.

3. Pope Benedict XV

Houlihan, Patrick J. "Pope Benedict XV and the forgotten campaign to end World War I." *America*, August 3, 2017, www.americamagazine.org/arts-culture/2017/08/03/pope-benedict-xv-and-forgotten-campaign-end-world-war-i.

Philpot, Terry. "World War I's Pope Benedict XV and the pursuit of peace." *National Catholic Reporter*, July 19, 2014, www.ncronline.org/news/justice/world-war-pope-benedict-xv-and-pursuit-peace.

Shaw, Russell. "Benedict XV: Forgotten pope of peace." *Our Sunday Visitor*, April 8, 2018, updated October 31, 2024, www.oursundayvisitor.com/benedict-xv-forgotten-pope-of-peace.

The Editors of Encyclopaedia Britannica. "Benedict XV." *Britannica*, last updated January 18, 2025, www.britannica.com/biography/Benedict-XV.

4. Pope Pius XI

Hollingsworth, Gerelyn. "On this day: Pope Pius XI." *National Catholic Reporter*, February 10, 2011, www.ncronline.org/blogs/ncr-today/day-pope-pius-xi.

The Editors of Encyclopaedia Britannica, "Pius XI." *Britannica*, last updated May 27, 2025. www.britannica.com/biography/Pius-XI.

5. Pope Pius XII

Bard, Mitchell. "The Vatican & the Holocaust: Pope Pius XII & the Holocaust." Jewish Virtual Library, accessed July 10, 2025, www.jewishvirtuallibrary.org/pope-pius-xii-and-the-holocaust.

Coppa, Frank J. "Pius XII." *Britannica*, last updated June 27, 2025, www.britannica.com/biography/Pius-XII.

Gussie, Kielce. "Legacy of Pope Pius XII lives on 66 years after his death." Vatican News, October 9, 2024, www.vaticannews.va/en/vatican-city/news/2024-10/pope-pius-xii-holocaust-jews-rome-peace.html.

6. Pope John XXIII

Cogley, John. "St. John XXIII." *Britannica*, last updated May 30, 2025, www.britannica.com/biography/Saint-John-XXIII.

"Pope John XXII 1958–1963." The Holy See, accessed July 10, 2025, www.vatican.va/content/john-xxiii/en/biography/documents/hf_j-xxiii_bio_16071997_biography.html.

"Saint John XXIII." Saint of the Day October 11, Franciscan Media, accessed July 10, 2025, https://www.franciscanmedia.org/saint-of-the-day/saint-john-xxiii/.

7. Pope Paul VI

"Biographical Profile Paul VI (1897–1978)," The Holy See, accessed July 14, 2025, www.vatican.va/content/paul-vi/en/biografia/documents/hf_p-vi_spe_20190722_biografia.html.

Heston, Edward Louis. "St. Paul VI." *Britannica*, last updated June 12, 2025, www.britannica.com/biography/Blessed-Paul-VI.

"Saint Paul VI." Church Leadership, Loyola Press, accessed July 14, 2025, www.loyolapress.com/catholic-resources/scripture-and-tradition/church-leadership/pope-paul-vi.

"Saint Paul VI." Saint of the Day September 26, Franciscan Media, accessed July 14, 2025, www.franciscanmedia.org/saint-of-the-day/saint-paul-vi.

The Editors of Encyclopaedia Britannica. "Second Vatican Council." *Britannica*, last updated June 7, 2025, www.britannica.com/event/Second-Vatican-Council.

8. Pope John Paul I

Gaetan, Victor. "Pope John Paul I's Legacy Is Rediscovered." *National Catholic Register*, July 10, 2024, www.ncregister.com/news/pope-john-paul-i-s-legacy-is-rediscovered-victor-gaetan.

Guernon, Mo. "John Paul I's 33-Day Papacy." *St. Anthony Messenger*, Franciscan Media, accessed July 15, 2025, www.franciscanmedia.org/st-anthony-messenger/john-paul-is-33-day-papacy.

Jones, Kevin J. "Nine things to know about John Paul I." Catholic News Agency, September 2, 2022, www.catholicnewsagency.com/news/252191/nine-things-to-know-about-john-paul-i.

Nixon, J. Peter. "Pope John Paul I, an alternative to the 'celebrity saint.'" *US Catholic*, August 31, 2022, uscatholic.org/articles/202208/pope-john-paul-i-an-alternative-to-the-celebrity-saint.

"Pope approves the heroic virtues of Servant of God Pope John Paul I." Vatican News, November 9, 2017, www.vaticannews.va/en/vatican-city/news/2017-11/pope-approves-the-heroic-virtues-of-servant-of-god-pope-john-pau.html.

Shaw, Russell. "John Paul I: The September pope." *Our Sunday Visitor*, September 2, 2018, updated October 31, 2024, www.oursundayvisitor.com/john-paul-i-the-september-pope.

The Editors of Encyclopaedia Britannica. "Blessed John Paul I." *Britannica*, last updated May 9, 2025, www.britannica.com/biography/Blessed-John-Paul-I.

9. Pope John Paul II

"Biographical Profile John Paul II (1920–2005)." *Booklet for the Celebration of the Canonization of Blesseds John XXIII and John Paul II*, The Holy See, April 27, 2014, www.vatican.va/content/

john-paul-ii/en/biografia/documents/hf_jp-ii_spe_20190722_biografia.html.

Blakemore, William B. "St. John Paul II." *Britannica*, last updated June 19, 2025, www.britannica.com/biography/Saint-John-Paul-II.

"St. John Paul II." Saint of the Day October 22, Franciscan Media, accessed July 22, 2025, www.franciscanmedia.org/saint-of-the-day/saint-john-paul-ii.

"John Paul II: A Biographical Sketch." Church Leadership, Loyola Press, accessed July 22, 2025, www.loyolapress.com/catholic-resources/scripture-and-tradition/church-leadership/pope-john-paul-ii-a-biographical-sketch.

10. Pope Benedict XVI

"Biography of His Holiness, Pope Benedict XVI." The Holy See, accessed July 22, 2025, www.vatican.va/content/benedict-xvi/en/biography/documents/hf_ben-xvi_bio_20050419_short-biography-old.html.

"Death of Pope Emeritus Benedict: his official biography." Vatican News, December 31, 2022, https://www.vaticannews.va/en/vatican-city/news/2022-12/pope-emeritus-benedict-xvi-official-biography.html.

Winfield, Nicole. "Benedict XVI, reluctant pope who chose to retire, dies at 95." Associated Press News, December 31, 2022, https://apnews.com/article/pope-benedict-xvi-a-life-remembered-ed6ddf20f696d84ffe0680e1ef0bab0f.

11. Pope Francis

Biography.com Editors and Catherine Caruso. "Pope Francis: Pope Francis was the 266th pope of the Roman Catholic Church whose historic election was followed by his embrace of social issues." Famous Religious Figures, Biography.com, updated April 22, 2025, www.biography.com/religious-figures/pope-francis.

"Biography of the Holy Father Francis." from *L'Osservatore Romano* 152, no. 61 (2014), The Holy See, www.vatican.va/content/francesco/en/biography/documents/papa-francesco-biografia-bergoglio.html.

Ostberg, René, Matt Stefon, and The Editors of Encyclopaedia Britannica, "Francis," *Britannica*, last updated July 19, 2025, www.britannica.com/biography/Francis-I-pope.

12. Pope Leo XIV

Ascension Team, "16 Fun Facts About Pope Leo XIV." Ascension Press, May 9, 2025, ascensionpress.com/blogs/articles/16-fun-facts-about-pope-leo-xiv.

"Biography of Pope Leo XIV, born Robert Francis Prevost." Vatican News, May 8, 2025, accessed July 22, 2025, www.vaticannews.va/en/pope/news/2025-05/biography-of-robert-francis-prevost-pope-leo-xiv.html.

Ostberg, René. "Leo XIV." *Britannica*, last updated July 21, 2025, https://www.britannica.com/biography/Leo-XIV.

Wiering, Maria. "Pope Leo XIV: A biographical timeline." Voices, *Catholic Standard*, May 9, 2025, www.cathstan.org/voices/pope-leo-xiv-a-biographical-timeline.

DOCUMENTS

1. Pope Leo XIII

Pope Leo XIII. "Rerum Novarum Encyclical of Pope Leo XIII on Capital and Labor." The Holy See, May 15, 1891, https://www.vatican.va/content/leo-xiii/en/encyclicals/documents/hf_l-xiii_enc_15051891_rerum-novarum.html.

Pope Leo XIII. "Graves de Communi Re Encyclical of Pope Leo XIII on Christian Democracy." The Holy See, January 18, 1901, https://www.vatican.va/content/leo-xiii/en/encyclicals/documents/hf_l-xiii_enc_18011901_graves-de-communi-re.html.

2. Pope Pius X

Pope Pius X. "E Supremi Encyclical of Pope Pius X on the Restoration of All Things in Christ." The Holy See, October 4, 1903, www.vatican.va/content/pius-x/en/encyclicals/documents/hf_p-x_enc_04101903_e-supremi.html.

Pope Pius X. "Singulari Quadam Encyclical of Pope Pius X on Labor Organizations." The Holy See, September 24, 1912, www.vatican.va/content/pius-x/en/encyclicals/documents/hf_p-x_enc_24091912_singulari-quadam.html.

Pope Pius X. "Il Fermo Proposito Encyclical of Pope Pius X on Catholic Action in Italy." The Holy See, June 11, 1905, www.vatican.va/content/pius-x/en/encyclicals/documents/hf_p-x_enc_11061905_il-fermo-proposito.html.

3. Pope Benedict XV

Pope Benedict XV. "Ad Beatissimi Apostolorum Encyclical of Pope Benedict XV Appealing for Peace." The Holy See, November

1, 1914, www.vatican.va/content/benedict-xv/en/encyclicals/documents/hf_ben-xv_enc_01111914_ad-beatissimi-apostolorum.html.

Pope Benedict XV. "Pacem, Dei Munus Pulcherrimum Encyclical of Pope Benedict XV on Peace and Christian Reconciliation." The Holy See, May 23, 1920, www.vatican.va/content/benedict-xv/en/encyclicals/documents/hf_ben-xv_enc_23051920_pacem-dei-munus-pulcherrimum.html.

4. Pope Pius XI

Pope Pius XI. "Ubi Arcano Dei Consilio Encyclical of Pope Pius XI on the Peace of Christ in the Kingdom of Christ." The Holy See, December 23, 1922, www.vatican.va/content/pius-xi/en/encyclicals/documents/hf_p-xi_enc_19221223_ubi-arcano-dei-consilio.html.

Pope Pius XI. "Quadragesimo Anno Encyclical of Pope Pius XI on Reconstruction of Social Order." The Holy See, May 15, 1931, www.vatican.va/content/pius-xi/en/encyclicals/documents/hf_p-xi_enc_19310515_quadragesimo-anno.html.

Pope Pius XI. "Divini Redemptoris Encyclical of Pope Pius XI on Atheistic Communism." The Holy See, March 19, 1937, www.vatican.va/content/pius-xi/en/encyclicals/documents/hf_p-xi_enc_19370319_divini-redemptoris.html.

5. Pope Pius XII

Pope Pius XII. "Summi Pontificatus Encyclical of Pope Pius XII on the Unity of Human Society." The Holy See, October 20, 1939, www.vatican.va/content/pius-xii/en/encyclicals/documents/hf_p-xii_enc_20101939_summi-pontificatus.html.

Pope Pius XII. "Summi Maeroris Encyclical of Pope Pius XII on Public Prayers for Peace." The Holy See, July 19, 1950, www.vatican.va/content/pius-xii/en/encyclicals/documents/hf_p-xii_enc_19071950_summi-maeroris.html.

Pope Pius XII. "Sertum Laetitiae Encyclical of Pope Pius XII on the Hundred and Fiftieth Anniversary of the Establishment of the Hierarchy in the United States." The Holy See, November 1, 1939, www.vatican.va/content/pius-xii/en/encyclicals/documents/hf_p-xii_enc_01111939_sertum-laetitiae.html.

6.Pope John XXIII

Pope John XXIII. "Ad Petri Cathedram Encyclical of Pope John XXIII on Truth, Unity and Peace in a Spirit of Charity." The Holy See, June 29, 1959, www.vatican.va/content/john-xxiii/en/encyclicals/documents/hf_j-xxiii_enc_29061959_ad-petri.html.

Pope John XXIII. "Mater et Magistra Encyclical of Pope John XXIII on Christianity and Social Progress." The Holy See, May 15, 1951, www.vatican.va/content/john-xxiii/en/encyclicals/documents/hf_j-xxiii_enc_15051961_mater.html.

Pope John XXIII. "Pacem in Terris Encyclical of Pope John XXIII on Establishing Universal Peace in Truth, Justice, Charity, and Liberty." The Holy See, April 11, 1963, www.vatican.va/content/john-xxiii/en/encyclicals/documents/hf_j-xxiii_enc_11041963_pacem.html.

7. Pope Paul VI

Pope Paul VI. "Populorum Progressio Encyclical of Pope Paul VI on the Development of Peoples." The Holy See, March 26, 1967, www.vatican.va/content/paul-vi/en/encyclicals/documents/hf_p-vi_enc_26031967_populorum.html.

Pope Paul VI. "Evangelii Nuntiandi Apostolic Exhortation of His Holiness Pope Paul VI." The Holy See, December 8, 1975, www.vatican.va/content/paul-vi/en/apost_exhortations/documents/hf_p-vi_exh_19751208_evangelii-nuntiandi.html.

8. Pope John Paul I

Pope John Paul I. "Address of His Holiness John Paul I to the Diplomatic Corps." The Holy See, August 31, 1978, www.vatican.va/content/john-paul-i/en/speeches/documents/hf_jp-i_spe_31081978_diplomatic-corps.html.

Pope John Paul I. "Urbi et Orbi Radio Message of His Holiness John Paul I." The Holy See, August 27, 1978, vatican.va/content/john-paul-i/en/messages/documents/hf_jp-i_mes_urbi-et-orbi_27081978.html.

Pope John Paul I. "Mass on the Occasion of Taking Possession of the Chair of the Bishop of Rome Homily of His Holiness John Paul I." The Holy See, September 23, 1978, www.vatican.va/content/john-paul-i/en/homilies/documents/hf_jp-i_hom_23091978.html.

John Paul I. "General Audience." The Holy See, September 6, 1978, www.vatican.va/content/john-paul-i/en/audiences/documents/hf_jp-i_aud_06091978.html.

John Paul I. "General Audience." The Holy See, September 20, 1978, www.vatican.va/content/john-paul-i/en/audiences/documents/hf_jp-i_aud_20091978.html.

John Paul I. "General Audience." The Holy See, September 27, 1978, www.vatican.va/content/john-paul-i/en/audiences/documents/hf_jp-i_aud_27091978.html.

9. John Paul II

Pope John Paul II. "Laborem Exercens." The Holy See, September 14, 1981, www.vatican.va/content/john-paul-ii/en/encyclicals/documents/hf_jp-ii_enc_14091981_laborem-exercens.html.

Pope John Paul II. "Sollicitudo Rei Socialis." The Holy See, December 30, 1987, www.vatican.va/content/john-paul-ii/en/encyclicals/documents/hf_jp-ii_enc_30121987_sollicitudo-rei-socialis.html.

Pope John Paul II. "Post-Synodal Apostolic Exhortation Reconciliation and Penance of John Paul II." The Holy See, December 2, 1984, www.vatican.va/content/john-paul-ii/en/apost_exhortations/documents/hf_jp-ii_exh_02121984_reconciliatio-et-paenitentia.html.

Pope John Paul II. "Centesimus Annus." The Holy See, May 1, 1991, www.vatican.va/content/john-paul-ii/en/encyclicals/documents/hf_jp-ii_enc_01051991_centesimus-annus.html.

Pope John Paul II. "Evangelium Vitae." The Holy See, March 25, 1995, www.vatican.va/content/john-paul-ii/en/encyclicals/documents/hf_jp-ii_enc_25031995_evangelium-vitae.html.

10. Pope Benedict XVI

Pope Benedict XVI. "Encyclical Letter Deus Caritas Est of the Supreme Pontiff Benedict XVI." The Holy See, December 25, 2005, www.vatican.va/content/benedict-xvi/en/encyclicals/documents/hf_ben-xvi_enc_20051225_deus-caritas-est.html.

Pope Benedict XVI. "Encyclical Letter Caritas in Veritate of the Supreme Pontiff Benedict XVI." The Holy See, June 29, 2009, www.vatican.va/content/benedict-xvi/en/encyclicals/documents/hf_ben-xvi_enc_20090629_caritas-in-veritate.html.

Pope Benedict XVI. "Post-Synodal Apostolic Exhortation Sacramentum Caritatis of the Holy Father Benedict XVI." The Holy See, February 22, 2007, www.vatican.va/content/benedict-xvi/en/apost_exhortations/documents/hf_ben-xvi_exh_20070222_sacramentum-caritatis.html.

11. Pope Francis

Pope Francis. "Encyclical Letter Laudato Si' of the Holy Father Francis on Care for our Common Home." The Holy See, May 24, 2015, www.vatican.va/content/francesco/en/encyclicals/documents/papa-francesco_20150524_enciclica-laudato-si.html.

Pope Francis. "Encyclical Letter Fratelli Tutti of the Holy Father Francis on Fraternity and Social Friendship." The Holy See, October 3, 2020, www.vatican.va/content/francesco/en/encyclicals/documents/papa-francesco_20201003_enciclica-fratelli-tutti.html.

Pope Francis. "Encyclical Letter Dilexit Nos of the Holy Father Francis on the Human and Divine Love of the Heart of Jesus Christ." The Holy See, October 24, 2014, www.vatican.va/content/francesco/en/encyclicals/documents/20241024-enciclica-dilexit-nos.html.

12. Pope Leo XIV

Pope Leo XIV. "Address of Pope Leo XIV to Members of the International Inter-Parliamentary Union." The Holy See, June 21, 2025, www.vatican.va/content/leo-xiv/en/speeches/2025/june/documents/20250621-giubileo-governanti.html.

Pope Leo XIV. "Message of the Holy Father for the 9th World Day of the Poor." The Holy See, June 13, 2025, www.vatican.va/

content/leo-xiv/en/messages/poor/documents/20250613-messaggio-giornata-poveri.html.

Pope Leo XIV. “Message of His Holiness Pope Leo XIV for the 10th World Day of Prayer for the Care of Creation 2025.” The Holy See, June 30, 2025, www.vatican.va/content/leo-xiv/en/messages/creation/documents/20250630-messaggio-giornata-curacreato.html.

Pope Leo XIV. “General Audience.” The Holy See, May 28, 2025, www.vatican.va/content/leo-xiv/en/audiences/2025/documents/20250528-udienza-generale.html.

Pope Leo XIV. “Homily of the Holy Father Leo XIV.” The Holy See, June 22, 2025, www.vatican.va/content/leo-xiv/en/homilies/2025/documents/20250622-omelia-corpus-domini.html.

Pope Leo XIV. “Homily of the Holy Father Leo XIV.” The Holy See, June 8, 2025, www.vatican.va/content/leo-xiv/en/homilies/2025/documents/20250608-omelia-pentecoste.html.

COVER IMAGES PERMISSIONS

Leo XIII, Pius X, Benedict XV, Pius XI, Pius XII, John XXIII, Paul VI, John Paul I: public domain, via Wikimedia.

John Paul II: Pope John Paul II smile FXD.jpg (cropped), Council of Ministers of the Republic of Poland (www.gov.pl), commons.wikimedia.org/wiki/File:Pope_John_Paul_II_smile_FXD.jpg, CC BY 3.0 PL (creativecommons.org/licenses/by/3.0/pl/deed.en).

Benedict XVI: Pope Benedict XVI, Berlin – 2011 (cropped).jpg (cropped), WDKrause, commons.wikimedia.org/wiki/File:Pope_Benedict_XVI,_Berlin_%E2%80%93_2011_(cropped).jpg, CC BY-SA 3.0 (creativecommons.org/licenses/by-sa/3.0/deed.en).

Francis: Franciscus in 2015.jpg (cropped), Casa Rosada (Argentina Presidency of the Nation) (www.casarosada.gob.ar), commons.wikimedia.org/wiki/File:Franciscus_in_2015.jpg, CC BY-SA 2.0 (creativecommons.org/licenses/by-sa/2.0/deed.en).

Leo XIV: Pope Leo XIV 3 (3x4 cropped).png (cropped), Edgar Beltrán, The Pillar, commons.wikimedia.org/wiki/File:Pope_Leo_XIV_3_(3x4_cropped).png, CC BY-SA 4.0 (creativecommons.org/licenses/by-sa/4.0/deed.en).

Ave Maria Press is an apostolate of the Congregation of Holy Cross, United States Province of Priests and Brothers. Ave is a nonprofit Catholic publishing ministry that serves the spiritual and formative needs of the Church and its schools, institutions, and ministers; Christian individuals and families; and others seeking spiritual nourishment.

Katie Prejean McGrady is a Catholic author and international speaker. She hosts the *Ave Explores* podcast and *The Katie McGrady Show* on Sirius XM's The Catholic Channel and she cohosts *Family Mass Prep* on the Hallow app with her husband, Tommy McGrady.

Shannon Wimp Schmidt is the content director of the ecumenical youth ministry collaboration TENx10, author of *Praying with the Psalms: 3-Minute Devotions for Lent and Holy Week 2025*, and coauthor of *Fat Luther, Slim Pickin's: A Black Catholic Celebration of Faith, Tradition, and Diversity*.

Eileen M. Ponder is executive editor of ministry resources at Ave Maria Press.

Founded in 1865, Ave Maria Press, a ministry of the Congregation of Holy Cross, is a Catholic publishing company that serves the spiritual and formative needs of the Church and its schools, institutions, and ministers; Christian individuals and families; and others seeking spiritual nourishment.

For a complete listing of titles from

Ave Maria Press

Sorin Books

Forest of Peace

Christian Classics

visit www.avemariapress.com